Reclaiming the Church

Other books by John B. Cobb, Jr.
published by Westminster John Knox Press

Matters of Life and Death
Process Theology as Political Theology

With D. R. Griffin
Process Theology: An Introductory Exposition

Reclaiming the Church

JOHN B. COBB, JR.

Westminster John Knox Press
Louisville, Kentucky

Book design by Jennifer K. Cox
Cover design by Pamela Poll
Cover illustration courtesty of PhotoDisk

First edition

Published by Westminster John Knox Press
Louisville, Kentucky

This book is printed on acid-free paper that meets the American National Standards Institute Z39.48 standard. ♾

PRINTED IN THE UNITED STATES OF AMERICA

97 98 99 00 01 02 03 04 05 06 — 10 9 8 7 6 5 4 3 2 1

Library of Congress Cataloging-in-Publication Data

Cobb, John B.
    Reclaiming the church / John B. Cobb, Jr. — 1st ed.
      p.   cm.
    ISBN 0-664-25720-8 (alk. paper)
    1. Church renewal.   2. United States—Church History—20th century.
    3. Christianity—Forecasting.   I. Title.
  BV600.2.C575   1997
  277.3'08929—dc20   96-36562

Contents

Preface

I have long lived with one foot in the field of professional theology; the other, in the church. I have become distressed about their growing separation and the results this has had for both. The church has come to identify theology with what professionals do. Since what professionals do has been increasingly determined by the norms of the university rather than by the needs of the church, the church has lost interest in what it understands to be "theology." Too often the result has been that the church has ceased to think about its own life in terms of its faith, a faith that has itself become vague and unconvincing. This is, I believe, the deepest cause of the decline of the oldline denominations.

Continuing decline is not, however, inevitable. We who have participated in, and contributed to, the decline can still make choices. The purpose of diagnosing a disease is to find a remedy. This book undertakes both to diagnose the current sickness of the church and to propose remedies.

If any of my readers should be persuaded of the need for the churches to renew their theological vocation and should seek more specific help in determining how that might happen, I refer them to two other books I have written. *Lay Theology* (Chalice Press) discusses the types of theological activity in which many members of the church could be involved and how churches might encourage and institutionalize it. *Becoming a Thinking Christian* (Abingdon Press) offers detailed suggestions for beginning the process of such reflection individually or, better, in small groups.

Thinking about this book began when I proposed to Westminster John Knox Press the publication of some lectures I had written over a period of years dealing with the present condition of the church. My editor Timothy Staveteig suggested that some of what I had included could be the nucleus of a useful volume. The resulting book includes ideas and some material from earlier lectures, but these have been reworked, making a more integrated book with much of the material newly written.

The introduction contains ideas first presented in Detroit, Michigan, at the fortieth annual meeting of the Continuing Congregational Churches. Chapter 1 draws on two unpublished lectures, one given at Garrett-Evangelical Theological Seminary in Evanston, Illinois, and the other at Queens College in Kingston, Ontario. Most of chapter 2 is adapted from a lecture given at Vanderbilt University Divinity School in Nashville, Tennessee, and subsequently published in *The Spire* ("Revisioning Ministry for a Revisioned Church," Summer/Fall 1992). Chapter 4 draws extensively from my Ainslie Lecture given in St. Louis, Missouri, and subsequently published in *Mid-Stream* ("The Unity of the Church and the Unity of Humanity," January 1995). In all instances I am grateful to my hosts for their graciousness as well as for stimulus and for encouragement to think that the ideas presented may have some value to others. With respect to the previously published material, I am grateful to *The Spire* and to *Mid-Stream* for permission to use it again in this quite different context.

Introduction
Spiritual Sickness as Lukewarmness

This book is written by a troubled member of an oldline denomination. I happen to be a United Methodist, and some of what I say will be based on my experience in that denomination. But the basic problems are present in other denominations as well, and it is to members of a wide range of such denominations that I address myself.

Our churches are sick. Statistical projections indicate that this is a sickness unto death. "Death" should not be taken literally. Great institutions rarely disappear without a trace. But we are moving from a situation in which we were not long ago thought of as "mainline" churches to one of marginality. To survive at the margin there is a danger that we will so change our character that what has been valuable in our churches will disappear. That is the "death" that is to be feared.

Since our decline is apparent to all, there is much discussion of its causes. The analysis of causes suggests prescriptions for stemming or reversing the tide of decay. If, for example, we are told that we are declining because we have become too liberal, then the prescription is to become more conservative. On the other hand, if the diagnosis is that we have been too reluctant to adopt contemporary language and ways of thought, the prescription is to become better connected with the culture. If we are told that we are too centralized, then we suppose that we need to give greater freedom to local congregations. If we decide that we are too intellectual or rational, we try to appeal more to the emotions. If the problem is that we do not think clearly enough or speak to the minds of people in our congregations, we try to become more scholarly. If our activity on social issues causes our weakness, we tone down these concerns. If it is our irrelevance to the real problems of the world that causes people to leave us, then we become more involved.

No doubt there is a grain of truth in all these accounts. But they remain superficial and of little help. We need to view ourselves more realistically in terms of the history that has formed us. We need also to analyze our present condition in the context of that history. Such analysis may suggest that our movement has had its day in the sun and must now, like so many historical movements, fade into obscurity. Or it may suggest that we are in a cyclical downswing that can be reversed. If so, it may also tell us what has brought about the downswing and how such downswings in the past have been turned around.

A basic assumption underlying the book is that the problem is spiritual or one of esprit. Movements flourish when their members are passionately committed. Christianity has flourished when Christians have been convinced that their faith is of supreme importance to them individually and collectively and also to the world. These convictions call forth deep personal commitment and willingness to sacrifice.

The results of such conviction have been ambiguous. We have become keenly aware, for example, of how often it has led to destructive treatment of those who do not share it, such as the Jews. Some who have suffered at Christian hands now rejoice that so many of us are now halfhearted. In that condition we are far less dangerous to them.

But the point is not that it is good or bad for Christians to have strong convictions. It is that without strong, shared Christian convictions among their members, churches decline. That is what is happening now.

If a community or institution is to be vital *as a church,* the convictions must be Christian. This does not mean that they must be convictions of which I as a Christian approve, or convictions that I as a Christian believe are responsibly derived from the Bible. The conviction may be, for example, that following a particular path ensures health and prosperity. I do not find this to be biblical or traditionally Christian nor a suitable innovation in the tradition. But if those who hold the conviction believe it to be at the heart of Christian faith, it can lead to vitality. Or again, many churches successfully encourage strong convictions supportive of patriarchy and, at least in principle, dangerous to Jews. I oppose these teachings, but that in no way denies that those who hold them believe them to be Christian and that they enhance the vitality of those churches in which they are widely shared.

The requirement that the strong convictions be shared is an important one and currently particularly difficult for oldline churches to achieve. If some members have strong convictions, but these are about concerns that seem unimportant or misguided to others, they cannot provide a basis for shared worship or action. There is a chance that the minority will be able to persuade a majority that has no strong conviction to accept their views for practical purposes at least, and this can lead to invigoration of a whole congregation. For example, if some are deeply convinced that the gospel calls for the inclusion of all types of people in the church (these days the issue is likely to be about homosexuals), and the majority have no comparably strong conflicting convictions, the congregation may be led to act on this conviction. After the loss of a few families, the congregation may be revitalized by its experience of acting on these partially shared convictions.

In the more common event, other members have contrary convictions. If both groups have a clear common understanding of the mission of the church, and if they can articulate it in such a way that they can understand and appreciate the opponents' views as sincere efforts to implement that mission, then the church can be invigorated by the ensuing debate, and it may remain united around still more fundamental commitments. But today in the oldline churches, this is rare. Occasionally, the congregation may divide. But more often the leadership holds it together out of institutional loyalty while losing most of those who have strong convictions and find that they can act on these better somewhere else. Those who remain are the lukewarm.

In the second and third chapters of the book of Revelation we find seven short letters to the seven churches of Asia. All are critical in some respect. The accusations addressed to some sound very serious. But the harshest rhetoric is reserved for the church of Laodicea, which is not accused of any wrongdoing. Its failure is that it is neither cold nor hot. Because it is lukewarm it will be spewed out of Christ's mouth.

This is bad news for us in the oldline churches today. As a group and on the whole we are lukewarm. We do good things. We serve real needs of real people. But we inspire no passion. We no longer even call for primary commitment to the gospel that we purport to serve. We are quite content if, among the priorities of our members, Christian faith comes in third or fourth, after family and employer and nation perhaps. We accept still lower rankings from many of our members with little complaint, glad for the small favor of occasional attendance and financial contributions.

Clearly a movement that ranks low among the priorities of its members cannot do much beyond the routine. It can, perhaps, allow groups of members who are more serious about their faith to act accordingly. An argument for local church autonomy today is that congregations can then express a seriousness about their faith that is absent in the denomination as a whole. But often it really means only that local churches cease to support what missional activities continue at regional or national levels.

In this condition the church cannot define the needs of the world from a Christian perspective and cannot order its activities to meeting those needs. Since it has few clear purposes beyond survival, its most pressing concern is the attraction of new members. To this end it adopts a marketing strategy. It finds out what people within commuting range want from a church, and it competes with other churches in the neighborhood to provide those services. Instead of condemning consumerism from a Christian perspective, churches accept it and adapt themselves to it. None of this activity is evil in itself, but there is nothing about such a church that calls for a high priority of commitment from its members or witnesses to that which is of ultimate importance. Even when the marketing strategy works for particular congregations, this does little to stem the decline of the oldline churches as a whole or even of the "successful" congregation.

This bleak picture is not descriptive of American Christianity as a whole. In some segments of contemporary American Protestantism the besetting sin is idolatry rather than lukewarmness. Such idolatry may be more dangerous both to members and to outsiders than is lukewarmness, but that is not our concern here. Idolatry is not the current sin of the oldline churches. In still other segments of the church, the problem may be deceptive expectations that cannot be fulfilled and lead to disillusionment and despair. That, too, may do more harm than lukewarmness. But the problem of the oldline churches is more commonly that expectations are too low; so this is not the problem to consider here. There may be segments of the church that are relatively free from any such serious problems. But their good fortune is only indirectly relevant to the concern here with the oldline churches.

This picture is intended, then, only to describe the oldline churches about which and for which this book is written. We need to look at ourselves realistically and diagnose our failures honestly. We need then to see whether we nevertheless have a continuing role to play that warrants our efforts to survive and even to grow. And if we decide that we do have such a role, then we need to consider what changes are needed if we are to reverse the current decay.

This book consists of five chapters. Chapter 1 asks why we have become lukewarm. It describes how the church recovered from earlier periods of lukewarmness and argues that a similar recovery would be possible today if the church would undertake to think through the issues that face it. Its seeming inability to do so is due, in large part, to the professionalization of theology, its location in the university, and its abandonment by the church.

Chapter 2 describes two proposals for responding to the decline of the church: renewal and transformation. It relates these proposals to the wider cultural situation in which much of what has long been taken for granted is coming to an end, and it shows how they respond to these endings and to the new beginnings that can now be discerned. It points out that the chief obstacle to movement in either of these directions is the inability of the church to think theologically.

Chapter 3 follows with an argument that though both renewal and transformation are needed, transformation is the more inclusive response. It affirms also that it is transformation that is most urgently needed today. It argues specifically for a transformation of our thinking about salvation and how this can renew wholehearted commitment in the church.

Chapter 4 shifts the focus to a different aspect of the church's current problem: the division between reformists and conservative traditionalists. A transformationist approach can achieve reconciliation in some, but certainly not all, cases. This transformationist approach also works beyond individual denominations to a new ecumenism that will seek reconciliation among the oldline churches, the post-Fundamentalists, and the Pentecostals. And finally, in a different way, it seeks reconciliation with other great religious communities.

The discerning reader will have noticed a tension throughout the preceding chapters. On the one hand, they call for the church to renew its theological vocation, leaving open what conclusions fresh reflection may reach. On the other hand, they are full of expressions of my own judgments about the kind of thinking that can save the church from lukewarmness and the accompanying decay. Chapter 5 renews the call for the church to think again, and it stresses that the most basic question on which it needs to think is the reality and nature of God. Much more extensively than elsewhere, however, it suggests, hopefully, where such thinking may lead today. Before embarking on this argument, however, the referent of *oldline churches* as used here should be specified.

First, the term "oldline" is limited here to the churches that were in existence at the beginning of the twentieth century. This distinguishes the oldline churches from the Fundamentalist and Pentecostal churches that have arisen in this century. (Relations to these are discussed in chapter 4.) The term "Protestant" excludes not only Orthodox and Catholics but also groups that have been clearly sectarian or ambivalent about their Christian identity, even if they were fully established at the beginning of the century. The account of oldline Protestant churches in this book has little relevance to Seventh-day Adventists, New Thought movements, Mormons, or Unitarian Universalists.

Second, other restrictions on the applicability of this account are not clearly implied by the designation "oldline Protestant." In fact, this book addresses only those oldline Protestant churches that have been involved ecumenically with one another and with the Orthodox and Catholics. Important denominations such as Southern Baptists and Missouri Synod Lutherans, as well as many other smaller denominations, have had a very different history and are in a very different situation than what is depicted here.

Finally, the churches here addressed—the ones that have become lukewarm—are predominantly white. This is said primarily to acknowledge that the situation within predominantly black churches is different. These churches also have problems, as well as strengths, but they require separate consideration. Also, there are many ethnic groups within the primarily white oldline denominations that have a quite different spirit from the white majority. The analysis in this book does not apply, for example, to Korean congregations in the Presbyterian and United Methodist denominations.

Since the account of oldline churches is not especially favorable, those omitted should not take offense! Some of the problems of these oldline churches, however, are shared by some of those who have been excluded from the classification presented here; hence members of other churches will not find this book entirely irrelevant. But to generalize even about the churches addressed here is risky. The account of the strengths and weaknesses of other traditions is for their members to provide.

1

Diagnosing the Loss
of Shared Convictions

The introduction argued that we are lukewarm because we do not have an understanding of Christian faith as supremely important either for ourselves or for the world. Obviously, this does not mean that no individual member of the oldline churches has such an understanding. I even claim to have one myself!

But no such understanding is widely operative in our collective work as congregations or denominations. There the topic is rarely even discussed. If it is raised, it is quickly silenced because of the danger of controversy. Hence there are no serious convictions available to generate enthusiasm for our churches as a whole. As a result, those who do understand the Christian faith to be of supreme importance experience the church as only one among a variety of contexts within which to express their faith rather than its fundamental bearer. Such private understandings do not change the basic situation of the churches.

There is, therefore, a lack of a shared sense of the primary importance of that to which the church witnesses. As long as this sense is lacking, the church cannot convincingly call for primary commitment or loyalty. It must inevitably settle for third, fourth, fifth, or sixth place in the priority system of most of its members. The temperature can at best be lukewarm. This cannot be changed unless there are powerful movements in which many members come to a shared conviction as to the primary, even ultimate, importance, for themselves and for the world, of the reality the church attests.

Such a shared conviction has been present in the oldline churches in the past. They have not always been lukewarm. Indeed, they would never have played their important role in American history if they had been lukewarm. A survey of our history, viewing it in terms of lukewarmness and passionate conviction, will help to illumine our present condition.

Challenge and Response in the Seventeenth and Eighteenth Centuries

In the early days of Protestantism in Europe, and in the early days of settlement in this country, lukewarmness was not the problem. The Pilgrims and the Puritans were far from lukewarm. They made great sacrifices for their faith and subordinated all other considerations to it. Roughly through the first half of the seventeenth century, we would be more likely to fault our Protestant forebears for fanaticism or idolatry than for lukewarmness. Nevertheless, in the second half of the seventeenth century and extending into the eighteenth century, lukewarmness became widespread. This remarkably abrupt shift in the role of Christianity in Europe and America requires explanation.

Much of the intense religious feeling in the first half of the seventeenth century focused on particular formulations of the faith. As a result, for half a century there were wars among competing Christian factions. The bloodshed was enormous. Increasingly, Christians viewed the passions that caused this situation as fanatical rather than as expressions of faith and began to look for a common ground among the competing factions. This was found in two places: nationalism and rationalism.

Christians on both sides of the conflicts felt loyalty and commitment to the well-being of their homelands. By shifting basic commitment from divisive religious institutions to political units, they could stop the killing among neighbors. Hence nation states took over primary responsibility from the churches. National governments were to regulate religious life within their boundaries and to prevent the animosities among Christian groups from leading to bloodshed. Each nation should respect the right of other nations to shape their own religious life. Thus nationalism arose in part as a way of controlling religious passions and their expressions.

The seventeenth century was also a time of enormous intellectual creativity and, especially, of scientific advances. For the first time since antiquity, Western Europeans believed that their reflections advanced upon and superseded those of the classical period. This meant that, in a very fundamental sense, reason replaced external authority as the basis for determining what should be believed, how society should be organized, and how people should act.

When scientists looked to Aristotle as their authority, there was no incongruity in looking to the Bible as religious authority. It would have seemed arrogant to appeal to current experience and reasoning against the wisdom of the ancients. But when scientists found that the ancients were wrong on many points, that through experiment and rational reflection they could come to a more comprehensive truth, the appeal to ancient scriptures became more dubious. Perhaps in religious and ethical matters as well, one should do one's own thinking.

The combination of the rise of nationalism and the emergence of rationalism did not bring an end to Protestantism, but it did bring an end to the social dominance of passionate commitment to Christian faith and the subordination of all else to this. Christianity was widely regarded as containing much wisdom that could be confirmed by reason and was supportive of the national good. Hence most of those committed primarily to nationalism and rationalism did not oppose it—at least in its Protestant form—as long as it performed its proper functions and avoided claiming too much for itself. They wanted Protestant Christianity to be lukewarm, and to a large extent it fulfilled their hopes. Lukewarm Christianity did not criticize nationalism and did not intrude on the primacy of reason.

Many individual Christians and small groups of Christians continued to believe in the primacy of the Christian faith. Some of them largely ignored the concerns of the nation, the cultural changes that had occurred, the claims of reason, and the new worldview of physics. On the other hand, there were those who affirmed the importance of the nation and embraced the claims of reason and the new worldview but integrated all this into an inclusive Christian vision. The latter overcame lukewarmness on a large scale in the Protestant churches.

The two most important influences in the revival of Christian conviction in the American churches were John Wesley and Jonathan Edwards. Both were thinkers as well as evangelists. Indeed, their evangelism expressed the deep confidence they had in the truth of Christianity as inclusive of all truth. Both integrated scriptural authority and reason rather than juxtaposing them. Both undertook to serve their communities, but in neither case would they allow a secular institution to define the good of the community for them. This they defined as Christians.

Together with many others they generated the evangelical movement that transformed the understanding of Christian faith in the English-speaking world. Through the change in the churches, they had a large impact on the whole of society. The faith of which they spoke was deeply personal but at the same time totally social. They did not focus on political action, but the reform of society to which they were both committed required such action among their followers. The antislavery movements in both England and the United States were deeply rooted in evangelicalism.

For millions of evangelicals, wholehearted commitment to Christ was the organizing and unifying principle of life. This did not require a defensive rejection of science or other advances in thought. Christian faith was felt to allow and include all of that. Hence, one did not need to divide one's loyalties between faith and knowledge. Also, to be a Christian was to be a good citizen. One did not have to divide one's loyalties between Christianity and the nation. A good Christian citizen did not give to the nation a loyalty equal to that given to Christ.

Of course, there were features of the evangelical teaching of the eighteenth century that are radically outdated today. The point here is not that they solved the problem of lukewarmness for all time, but that they showed how it could be overcome in a particular historical situation. The attempt to continue just this form of evangelicalism in our changed situation, by ignoring the issues raised in the past two centuries, produces an "evangelicalism" that is not truly good news and lacks the authenticity of the original form.

Challenge and Response in the Nineteenth Century

The nineteenth-century challenges to inherited Christian thinking were more varied and drastic than those of the eighteenth century. Three challenges were especially important: the rise of historical consciousness, focusing especially on the quest of the historical Jesus; the appearance of evolutionary thinking, first in biology, but then more inclusively as a general worldview; and the sociological reflection occasioned by the Industrial Revolution and the new class structure it brought into being.

The original evangelicalism was based on an open-minded and open-spirited embrace of the science and reason of the eighteenth century, but it tended to close itself to the new challenges of the nineteenth. The evangelicalism that had led in the struggle against slavery and in other social causes became increasingly individualistic and inward-looking in the latter part of the century. Inevitably, it lost the power to evoke wholehearted commitment from the more thoughtful and sensitive segment of the population including many who continued their membership in the churches. It tended to be defensive in the face of new challenges. Lukewarmness returned.

Despite the complexity of the new challenges, toward the end of the nineteenth century effective responses emerged. Evolutionary thought was accepted and the Bible was interpreted in radically historical, even evolutionary, ways. The new historical understanding of Jesus displayed him as relevant to the sociological situation produced by industrialization. A new piety arose that involved a deeply inward commitment to working with God to bring into being the kingdom of God. This was understood in terms of peace among nations, justice for the poor, universal education, and the spread of democracy.

In short, the new knowledge was assimilated into a comprehensive vision that was fundamentally Christian. To give oneself to the cause of Jesus did not involve disputing well-established knowledge of either history or biology. On the contrary, this knowledge supported it. Working with God to bring about God's kingdom could call for wholehearted devotion, and it evoked that from millions of oldline Protestants.

This commitment to the kingdom of God informed religous education. It provided the context for much of the world missionary movement of the late nineteenth and early twentieth centuries. It gave birth to the ecumenical movement in both the United States and the world. It led to great expectations of winning the world for Christ.

The social gospel shaped much of the healthiest part of church life in this country until World War II. Since then it has declined. It did not provide an adequate basis for dealing with the realities of that war or with the waves of challenges to Christian faith that have followed it. But like the evangelical movement a century earlier, it shows what is needed. Unless the Christian faith can provide the basis for assimilating the truth of the new challenges of the twentieth century into a whole that is communicable to many, and unless Christians can point convincingly to what this new vision requires, oldline Protestantism will relapse more and more into lukewarmness—and death.

Of course, this does not apply to all forms of Christianity. Christian faith can continue to claim total loyalty among those who are willing to ignore or deny the new (and old) challenges. This may have great value for individual believers, but for society as a whole, it poses a threat. This form of Christianity is not truly good news. Even so, it may be that the next inclusive Christian vision will arise, not in the churches that have been, thus far, most open to the challenges but in those that have not yet faced them. One more often finds in them the wholehearted commitment apart from which an adequate response to the new challenges is not possible. It is not for us to dismiss these churches, or the authenticity of the faith they nourish, when our own is so lukewarm!

Challenge and Response in the Twentieth Century

What are, then, the new challenges of the twentieth century to which neither the evangelicalism of the eighteenth century nor the social gospel of the nineteenth century is adequate? As noted, World War II ended the ability of the social gospel to evoke wholehearted commitment in the American churches. It had identified the kingdom of God too much with the fulfillment of Enlightenment ideals. It shared in the Eurocentrism of the time. It had also underestimated the power of sin and evil to block the movement toward the kingdom of God. Some of these weaknesses had been noted already after World War I by leading theologians, so that the social gospel had lost its status as cutting edge theology decades before it lost its role in the churches.

However, this alone would not have ended its contribution. Reinhold Niebuhr was the major American critic of the social gospel, but his work was as much a deepening of that gospel as a rejection. His influence both before and after World War II was enormous, and it provided a way for many to continue wholehearted commitment to Christian faith. Unfortunately, its subtlety and pessimism about permanent improvements in the human situation hindered its translation into church programs and so prevented it from sustaining the full force of the earlier social gospel. In any case it did not overcome the

Eurocentrism whose inappropriateness has become increasingly evident since World War II.

The ability of the social gospel to invigorate the churches was weakened by the great wars and by critical theological discussion. But it was the new challenges that began to emerge in the sixties that have led to the present demoralized state of oldline churches. The new challenges differed from most of those in the nineteenth century in a very important way.

The earlier challenges primarily questioned the credibility of Christian faith. Darwinian evolutionary theory seemed to contradict biblical teaching and required a rethinking of the Christian doctrine of creation and of the relation of human beings to the remainder of creation. This demanded also a new, critical interpretation of the Bible. Critical biblical study undercut established beliefs not only about the Bible in general and its inspiration, but also about who Jesus was, what he taught, and how he was understood by the earliest Christians.

These were radical changes in Christian thinking, but I have argued that by the end of the nineteenth century a response adequate to the needs of the churches was being made. The Christianity that emerged was different from any that had existed before, but it was not less rooted in the Bible or less able to call forth full devotion to Christ.

The twentieth century has continued to assault the credibility of Christian beliefs, but the new challenge has been to its value. On topic after topic, open-minded Christians have been forced to recognize that Christian faith has done great harm. Previously, Christians attributed the evil done by Christians to their failure to live up to their own ideals. But now it is clear that it has resulted not only from our failure to live up to our highest ideals but also from our conformity to them.

The response to such challenges has led many sensitive Christians to reject the faith altogether. Why subscribe to a set of beliefs that do great harm? Others, however, are convinced that they are called to participate in the repentance of the church rather than to abandon it. This entails both regret for the past crimes of Christianity and the effort to change. The oldline churches have gone furthest in confession and redirection, but the result has been decline rather than revitalization.

Some of our losses are inevitable. During a period dominated by repentance, few outsiders are drawn to a community. Human beings are more attracted to successful achievement than to acknowledgment of failure and wrongdoing. On the other hand, the response has enabled many to remain in oldline churches who otherwise would have been driven out of Christianity altogether.

The question is now, Why have the churches that have responded most to the challenges become the most halfhearted, the most lukewarm? That question requires a more detailed answer. Let us look at three examples of the challenges and responses in order to formulate a somewhat nuanced explanation. There have been many other challenges, so that responding adequately to these three would not solve all problems. We will return in chapter 2 to a more comprehensive account of the context within which the church must think through to a new response. But these examples will serve to indicate where the problem lies.

Anti-Judaism

In the 1960s Jews and Christians finally began to analyze in a public way the role of Christianity in preparing the ground for the Holocaust. By the end of that decade a considerable literature by Christians on Christian anti-Judaism had appeared. Gradually the fact was assimilated that Christian teaching, beginning with the New Testament itself, has been anti-Jewish. It became clear that the climate of anti-Jewish feeling generated by this teaching had made possible the genocide that so shocked the world.

So far as I know, there had been no previous experience of this kind in religious history. A religious community participated in displaying its own guilt before the world. Since what it had done was presented *as guilt,* the act was already one of repentance. And various church bodies officially stated their regret and their intention to avoid continuing to contribute to the climate of anti-Judaism.

There have been efforts to remove obviously anti-Jewish language from the life of the church generally and to engage in practical steps to recognize the value and validity of contemporary Judaism. Thousands of Jewish-Christian dialogues have involved tens of thousands of lay Christians and clergy at many levels. National and international organizations work to change agelong stereotypes.

Perhaps most important, within the oldline denominations few *want* to continue teachings or practices once they recognize their anti-Jewish nature. To show that a doctrine or practice is anti-Jewish is to demonstrate the need for change. To *this* extent repentance is almost universal.

Goodwill and good intentions along with deletion of offensive language and extended personal contacts are an important gain. The old-line churches have some right to feel proud about what they have done. Why, then, has this experience contributed instead, or at least also, to the lukewarmness that is their pressing problem?

It does so for theological reasons. The ways in which in the past the churches called for commitment to Jesus Christ are now recognized to have a dark side in their implications for Jews. To speak of Jesus Christ as the only Lord and Savior implies that those who rejected and continue to reject him deny their Lord and refuse salvation. But what is Christian faith in Christ if it does not affirm him as Lord and Savior?

A number of theologians have worked extensively on this problem. There are answers—good ones, I think. If the churches embraced these answers clearly and enthusiastically, they immediately could call their members to devoted service and loyal commitment and also make it clear that this did not deny to Jews the truth and validity of their beliefs and claims.

But that would require extensive theological discussion and debate throughout the churches. This has not occurred. Without such theological repentance to accompany the moral repentance, the best that can be done is to tone down the traditional rhetoric, reduce commitment to what it says, and hope that what remains will do little harm. That is a recipe for lukewarmness.

Feminism

The most pervasive recent impact on the church has been made by feminism. There have been earlier waves of feminism going back into the nineteenth century, and these made some dent on the oldline churches. A few women, here and there, were ordained. But ministry remained a male profession, and the fundamentally patriarchal character of the church was not affected.

The feminism of the past quarter century has been a quite different story. It has been far more sustained in its insistence on equality for women in the church, and the oldline churches have opened their doors for this equality. In many seminaries, as many women as men are now studying for ministry, perhaps more, when we restrict ourselves to the churches here in view. Resistance to women ministers in congregations is eroding. The number of women in positions of high authority is considerable and is increasing. There is a long way to go before the numbers of men and women at all levels are in balance, but the speed of movement in that direction is remarkable.

Christian feminists, of course, are interested not only in job opportunities within the church, but also in being fully included in the self-understanding of the church. They rightly point out that this does not take place as long as their presence is obscured by the absence of the feminine pronoun in reference to them. However often we say that the pronoun "he" means both "he" and "she," it continues to evoke the image of the male. The oldline churches have heard this point, and on the whole they are changing their rhetoric accordingly.

Far more difficult is language about God. Feminist Christians argue that as long as God is named only in masculine language, God will be conceived as male. If the supreme power is seen as male and worshiped as such, the human male will appear to be more like God than is the female. Since so many Christians have drawn these patriarchal conclusions in the past, the connection between language and practice cannot responsibly be denied. But changing language about God is peculiarly difficult. Male terms, such as "Lord" and "Father," are so pervasive of the Bible, the tradition, and the liturgy, that they can neither be removed nor equally balanced with female imagery in the short term.

Furthermore, there is great resistance to change. Many not only address God as their heavenly Father but also think of God as such. The abandonment of the language of "Father," or the equal inclusion of the language of "Mother" is not a terminological change alone, but also a religious one. This is, of course, the feminists' point. Christianity has been, and is, patriarchal through and through.

Many feminists simply reject Christianity for this reason. They do not believe that it is subject to such a fundamental change as to cease to be patriarchal. On the other hand, Christian feminists call for just that change. They believe that a change of rhetoric will communicate different images to our children, images that will transform Christian piety and spiritual understanding, and they believe that the transformed Christianity will be more, not less, Christian.

Despite great resistance, change is occurring. As the oldline churches produce new hymnals, the patriarchal images of God are giving way to greater balance. As this happens in hymns, it can and will happen in other parts of worship. Eventually, the way members of these churches think about God will change.

Perhaps the other changes for which feminists call can occur only as Christian thinking about God becomes less patriarchal. They do not want simply to serve in the roles that males have established. They understand leadership and power differently, and they want to develop less hierarchical patterns of organization. Here, too, a few churches have experimented. But we do not yet know what the full inclusion of feminist insights would mean for the life of the church or whether the repentance of the oldline churches will ever go far enough for us to find out.

Indeed, we do not yet know whether a genuinely feminist Christianity is possible. Many, both post-Christian feminists and anti-feminist Christians, believe that it is not. They do not deny that the oldline churches can do much to rectify the injustices that have been inflicted on women in the past. But they do not believe that the church can change in its basic way of imaging God or ordering its life. To these issues we will return in later chapters.

What is important here is that the oldline churches have repented of their extreme sexism and are exploring how far such repentance can and should lead. Few questions can be more important for the future of Christianity. Whatever the final answer, the leadership of the oldline churches in this experiment is impressive.

Why then has the impact of feminism on the oldline churches also contributed to the current malaise? The answer is, again, that repentance has been practical and ethical, and in this case also rhetorical, but not theological. Feminism raises questions not just about the language to use about God but about the nature of God. It challenges both traditional philosophical theism and some ideas that come to expression in biblical images. Whereas its proposals about changes in language have forced discussion and action in the churches, its theological assertions have not. We are left with an increasing sense that no one knows, or much cares, who or what "God" is. The church cannot call for ultimate devotion to such an uncertain entity. In chapter 5 we will return to this fundamental theological problem.

The Ecological Crisis

In the mid–sixties a Presbyterian layman, Lynn White, Jr., gave a lecture in which he stated that the way the Bible was read in the West played a key role in sowing the seeds of the ecological crisis. His point was that in the Western church the Bible was taken to give human beings dominion over all other creatures and thereby to justify the technological manipulation of the environment for narrowly human ends. This freedom to control opened the door to highly destructive practices that were not criticized or even noticed by the church.

This charge against Christianity was more particularized than the ones considered above about Christian anti-Judaism and patriarchalism. White did not see comparable developments in Eastern Orthodoxy. Even in the West he found resources for going in a different direction. Furthermore, the encouragement of a dominating technology is not uniformly regarded as evil today. Nevertheless, partly because of the influence of White's lecture, many of those who were awakened to the ecological crisis in the late sixties assumed that Christianity was part of the problem and turned their backs on it.

White's thesis, combined with a more general attack on Christianity from ecologically concerned people, evoked an extensive Christian literature. Some of this literature was simply defensive, arguing that Christianity was innocent of any wrongdoing. But even in this literature, new interpretations of key biblical passages emerged. There was unwitting, and perhaps unwilling, "repentance."

Many Christians recognized that, indeed, Western Christian teaching, especially in the modern period, had been guilty of alienating human beings from the earth. To some extent the very openness to science and historical scholarship I celebrated above had led to a dualist vision of the human and the natural. These Christians saw that there were roots of this alienating dualism in the Bible, but that more adequate appraisal of the Bible provides grounds for attitudes and practices that are far more promising. They called for intentional repentance and strong support by the church for the public changes that are needed.

The process of repentance of the churches for their neglect of the natural world can be observed quite dramatically in the recent history of the World Council of Churches. At the time of the 1972 United Nations meeting on the environment, held at Stockholm, the World Council was not ready to participate. It feared that environmental concerns would distract from its focus on justice. But three years later at its Assembly in Nairobi, it recognized the need to take the environment seriously. Previously it had spoken of its commitment to "a just and participatory society." At Nairobi it added "sustainable." The churches are to work for "a just, participatory, and sustainable society."

During the following seven years there was a great deal of study and reflection about the meaning and implications of sustainability. The newness of the term increased attention to it. However, at the next assembly, at Vancouver in 1982, this bore little fruit. The idea of sustainability virtually disappeared from the discussion.

There were two reasons for this. First, the World Council tried hard to have grassroots delegates rather than only those accustomed to attending ecumenical and international meetings. As a result something like 85 percent of the delegates had never taken part in any World Council activity before coming to Vancouver. They were largely unaware of what had happened at Nairobi or in the subsequent meetings. What was shown was that when Christians are not directed to attend to the natural world, their habits are such that they ignore it.

Second, the cold war threatened to become hot. Delegates from the First and Second Worlds were preoccupied with the issue of peace. Meanwhile, Third World delegates emphasized that peace between the First and Second Worlds was not the pressing concern of hundreds of millions of people living in degrading poverty and oppression. The issue posed to the assembly was the relation of peace and justice.

The assembly was about to close with a fine statement on peace and justice when someone proposed adding the phrase "the integrity of creation." Once again, when directly asked to consider the natural world, Christians responded affirmatively. With little discussion the phrase was added. The churches are now directed to work for "Justice, Peace, and the Integrity of Creation."

This worked out well. The sustainability of societies remains an anthropocentric concern. That is better than no concern for the environment at all! But it does not address directly the problem of Christian anthropocentrism to which White had called attention. "The integrity of creation" breaks with anthropocentrism. Furthermore, the freshness of the term and its lack of definition set off a new flurry of activity in the World Council, keeping the discussion of the relation of Christians to the remainder of creation alive.

The development of World Council thinking from indifference to nature to going beyond anthropocentrism can be paralleled in a number of denominational statements. At the level of official position, repentance has come a long way. At the level of liturgy and preaching in local churches, less change has occurred, and much remains to be done. At the level of mobilizing the church for effective action, most of the work lies in the future.

Here, again, the oldline churches can be proud of their leadership in responding to a challenge of penultimate importance. Here the response *has* been theological, and it has moved far in the right direction. It turns out that recovering the doctrines of the creation of the natural world, of its intrinsic worth, and of human responsibility in and for it has not been as threatening as changing the ways we think about Christ and God. Hence progress has been greater, and the contribution to lukewarmness less.

Nevertheless, even here much of the theological work still has not been done, or at least it has not been assimilated into the churches. The ethical message that exploitation is wrong and that care of the earth is required has been heard and is finding its way occasionally into the pulpit. The extent to which this changes, or can change, our understanding of ourselves and of salvation is hardly noticed. On the whole, the "environment" is added as another special cause to be placed alongside others and emphasized once a year on Earth Day. This does little to restore wholeheartedness.

Creation spirituality shows the much deeper changes that follow when the implications of these theological shifts are worked through. For this reason it has the capacity to evoke a wholehearted commitment from those who understand the seriousness of the Earth's problem. It shows also how change in this respect also alters the understanding of Christ and God in ways that go far to solve the problems raised by the recognition of Christian anti-Judaism and by feminism. But creation spirituality is not discussed in the churches. It would be controversial, and for the sake of avoiding controversy, or simply from the habit of not thinking theologically, the churches sink further and further into lukewarmness.

The three challenges presented above omit the one to which the oldline churches have given the greatest attention: confrontation with their long acquiescence in racism in society and in their own structures and practices. The reason for this omission is that the response to this challenge required only taking established beliefs and commitments seriously. Change was painful and sometimes costly, but it did not contribute to the growing lukewarmness. If anything it has provided some of the residue of passion and commitment that still keep oldline churches alive.

The Professionalization of Theology

Despite the negative consequences for the oldline churches of what they have done in responding to the other challenges of the twentieth century, their responses have been an important contribution to Christianity and the world as a whole. Without these responses, Christianity would appear generally insensitive to its sins and unwilling to repent of them. Such a Christianity would not only appear but also be a threat to others and to the planet. Other branches of Christianity have responded to one or more of these challenges, but oldline Protestants have often led the way, and without their work there would have been less response from others. The contribution of the oldline churches is to be celebrated.

Furthermore, if this analysis is accurate, a move from a situation of lukewarmness to a new vitality is possible. Much of the needed theological work has been done. Creation spirituality stands out because it has institutionalized its outreach and has affected tens of thousands of people, many of whom are members of oldline Protestant churches.

If other proposals for rethinking Christian faith in light of the challenges of the twentieth century can capture the imagination of lay people and ministers as effectively as has this one, the needed theological discussion may take place even if it is not encouraged by church leaders. If this should happen, then the oldline Protestant churches might make again a contribution to the larger church and society analogous to that which they made through the evangelical and social gospel movements.

Nevertheless, a move from where we now are to where we need to be will be very difficult to make. That is not because the makings of a convincing understanding of faith for our time are not available. It is because the church has lost the capacity to appropriate what it is offered. This is partly because to do so would be controversial and divisive. But more deeply, it is because the church has no organs of thought. It has turned these over to the university, which has transformed them into academic disciplines. It is time to reflect on how the church came to abandon its theological vocation.

The answer here, too, is found in recent history. What is the difference between our situation and that of a century ago? Why was the church able, toward the end of the nineteenth century, to respond effectively to the challenges of that time, whereas it has not been able to respond in a similar way to the challenges of the second half of the twentieth century?

A convenient answer might be that our challenges are more difficult. That may, or may not, be true. Perhaps greater theological sophistication is required now, but by itself that would explain little. Far greater theological sophistication is now available. The number of highly trained scholars teaching in oldline Protestant seminaries is far greater than at the end of the nineteenth century. Furthermore, as I have noted, individuals have done much of the work that is needed in order to reaffirm Christian faith as of decisive importance in a way that does not continue to have the negative consequences of past formulations. The problem lies in the gap now existing between theology and church life, a gap that did not exist to any comparable extent a century ago.

The pastors who initiated the fundamental theological changes involved in the social gospel were able to do so because they understood themselves to be responsible for articulating the meaning of the gospel to their people. They knew themselves, in this basic sense, to be theologians. Many lay Christians joined them in redefining salvation as social, in a fresh reading of the Bible, and in acceptance of an evolutionary worldview. They did not find it presumptuous to engage in these theological tasks.

Today, the situation is different. The vast majority of lay people and even most pastors deny that they are theologians. For them, theology is something that is done by scholars in universities and theological schools. Lay people and pastors do not understand themselves as responsible to think as Christians. Such responsibility as they accept is for the operation of the church, the adjudication of disputes that arise within it, and moral judgments in response to issues posed to them, usually by the secular world.

In short, what has happened is the professionalization of theology. This began in the late nineteenth century, but even in the first half of the twentieth century the process had not gone far enough to shape the churches' basic relation to theology. Lay people and ministers continued to take responsibility for their Christian beliefs. Obviously, most of their theological discussions had limited scholarly value, but they shaped popular convictions in ways that were often healthy.

The situation was quite different in Germany. There theology had long been professionalized, and in that capacity it played a leading role in the great universities that were the wonder of the scholarly world. Would-be scholars from the United States made pilgrimages to Germany and stood in awe of what they found there. Viewing the American theological discussion from the perspective of what they experienced in Germany, they could only be appalled by its lack of historical depth, scholarly rigor, and intellectual sophistication. Gradually they began to reshape theological education in the United States.

The formal shift was accompanied by a material one. In the period between the two world wars, German-language theology defined faith over against culture. It brought to this analysis a devastating critique of major trends in nineteenth-century German Protestantism, including movements within it analogous to the social gospel. And, of course, this was carried out with characteristic German rigor and historical erudition. The American social gospel, and in general the beliefs that informed the American churches, appeared highly vulnerable to this critique. When the depression finally assaulted American self-confidence, this crisis theology or Neo-Orthodoxy was imported into the United States and established in the East Coast seminaries as the norm for what theology should be.

The impact of this event was enormous. It broke the power of the social gospel to shape the lives of the churches. But even more important, it reduced the possibility of similar movements arising in the church by redefining theology. For the Neo-Orthodox Europeans, theology was a *Wissenschaft,* that is, an academic discipline. That did not mean for them that it failed to address the church. Far from it. But it did mean that it had to measure up to academic standards in order to do so. These standards were rigorous indeed, and few laypersons or pastors were able to participate in the shaping of theology. At best most of the pastors could follow the discussion among the professionals and be informed by that. They could also work out some of the implications of theology for the life of the church and the world.

After World War II, ministry in the United States in general was professionalized. This involved extensive expansion of theological schools and provided a place for a much larger number of academically trained theologians to work. Their academic training oriented them to the German model.

Thus, during the past fifty years, theology in the United States also became an academic discipline. Some theologians accepted and internalized the German model, immersing themselves in the history of German theological scholarship and entering into that discussion. Others developed standards of scholarship of a different sort, more congenial to the American scene. But neither group related to the American church the way German theology related to the German church.

This was not, on the whole, a conscious choice by those who pursued the new academic discipline in the United States. The context was simply different. Throughout the nineteenth century, church and state had developed in Germany an intricate relation to the discipline of theology in the universities. Theologians were public figures who weighed their words with expectation of significant impact. Pastors had been educated in the methods by which these theologians developed new theories out of the tradition. Although few were able to contribute to the discussion, most were quite able to follow it and to have informed opinions about it. They knew that theology was important. Theologians saw their work as directly in the service of preaching, and preaching was the main function of pastors.

None of this applied in the United States. The only audience for the new academic theology was the community of professional theologians, their students, and a few interested ministers. Furthermore, whereas in Germany there was one ongoing discussion in a single community of theologians, the situation in the United States was far more pluralistic. Interested pastors could not learn where *the* theological discussion was heading, since there were many such discussions going on, with little interaction.

Added to this was that most Americans thought the most advanced theological work continued to be in Germany. When pastors wanted to know what was going on in theology, the most natural response was to describe the German scene. A major function of American academic theologians was to keep themselves and their students abreast of developments in the German-language world. That was all very well, but the cultural and historical difference between the American and the central European churches meant that application of German developments to the American scene tended to be quite artificial. The interest of American pastors in theology as now defined rapidly waned.

For a short period, it seemed that there would be a role for American theology outside the theological schools in the burgeoning programs in religion in American colleges and universities. However, this did not work out. American colleges and universities wanted the study of religion but not the faithful articulation of the beliefs of one particular community, especially the Christian one. American theology was restricted to schools of theology.

The one clear function of the American theologian was to teach future pastors and, perhaps, future teachers of pastors. The question was what to teach. On the whole, the judgment was that students needed to be made aware of the changes that had occurred in theology through the centuries and be brought abreast of the contemporary discussion. That discussion was defined as the academic one, especially in Germany. This was an enormous task that could not be carried out well in the few courses available. But it was possible to make pastors aware that the notions they had gleaned, growing up in the American church, were naive, and that the goal of functioning as theologians themselves was attainable only by going on for a doctoral degree.

There remained the question of what pastors would preach. They could not preach simply *about* what professional theologians had to say. They must have some convictions of their own to share with their congregations. The academic theologians responded to this in two ways. Some tried to confront students with the plurality of academically responsible options and encourage them to choose among them or to create their own syntheses; others offered their own conclusions and tried to persuade students to accept those.

Although individual students might catch a vision of what their ministry could and should be about from these exposures, this kind of teaching did not contribute to a new shared theological understanding that could give direction to the church as a whole. For the most part, practical issues of preaching, management, and counseling were dealt with in specialized courses informed by different perspectives, ones that might or might not have a theological cast. And most ministers, for most purposes, fell back on the popular notions they brought with them to seminary, only now knowing that these could not be taken seriously as "theology."

There are two additional features of the acceptance of university norms for theology that have worked against its relevance in the church. First, academic disciplines function best when their subject matters are narrowly defined. This makes it possible to develop appropriate methodologies of greater rigor. Hence the disciplinary organization of knowledge leads to divisions and subdivisions of disciplines. In the case of theology, it was separated from ethics in the period soon after World War II. This encouraged theologians to focus on more purely theoretical questions with little concern for their relation to practice. In the new discipline of Christian ethics, it led to intense concern with its self-definition as a separate discipline. Questions of methodology long predominated over efforts to help the church think wisely about the social issues with which it had to deal.

Second, as theology increasingly became a discipline in the American seminary, the constructive task itself became suspect. The university understands historical study and hermeneutical method. At best it tolerates constructive thinking. Hence, there is a tendency for seminary professors of theology to take less responsibility for the ongoing development of theology. It suffices to be a good student and critic of theology, who can pass on to one's students a critical understanding of what theologians have said. Hence, whereas earlier the professors at least felt responsibility to help their students come to some resolution of theological issues for themselves, this can no longer be taken for granted. Those most fully socialized into the disciplinary habit of mind find that purpose uncongenial.

The transformation of Christian thinking into a university discipline was not forced on the church by the university. It was chosen by the church and by its theologians. Theologians want to function according to disciplinary norms. This is partly so as to be able to function in university contexts. But even those in freestanding seminaries internalize these norms. Obviously they find a great deal of satisfaction in functioning in this way.

The rewards are, indeed, great.

1. There is the satisfaction involved in feeling that the quality of what one is doing is high. Americans who studied in Germany were long disturbed by the superficiality and naïveté of what was being called

theology in the United States. To bring theological reflection up to, or at least toward, the level standardized in Germany has seemed inherently important. Success in this endeavor has changed the global theological scene, with Americans now working almost as equals alongside German scholars.

2.   There is the intellectual freedom granted by the university. As long as one thinks responsibly, as judged by university standards, one is free to allow one's study to carry one where it will. Conclusions that are unpopular in the church can receive a fair hearing, and those who voice them are protected. Their jobs are secure. Theologians who have watched what has happened to compeers who are more directly under the control of churches have reason to appreciate the university and its guarantees of academic freedom. While the Roman Catholic Church and the Southern Baptists sharply narrow the parameters of what their theologians can write or teach, those ensconced in non-Catholic universities, or in oldline denominational seminaries where university standards prevail, remain free.

3.   There is the intellectual stimulation available from an institution in which research takes place in so many disciplines. One is treated as an equal as long as one's discipline can demonstrate that it subscribes to and fulfills university expectations. One can teach and learn in free interplay with one's peers in other disciplines.

4.   There is a sense that keeping theology alive in this context is itself an important mission of the church. In general, university professors are skeptical of the intellectual substance of church beliefs and pronouncements. They tend to identify Christianity with popular superstition or as a fossil that retains outdated ideas. It is satisfying to counter these impressions by representing a tradition within Christianity that has remained in the forefront of scholarship and intellectual life.

5. The subject matter of the discipline of theology is intrinsically interesting. Even if one were not a Christian who experienced the intellectual struggle as existentially important, one would have to acknowledge its value. Questions of ultimate meaning are being probed through a complex of historical and philosophical questions, interesting in themselves, but more interesting when brought into juxtaposition with one another.

6. There are opportunities within the university, including the seminary, to help students with their personal struggles for faith in a time when the dominant intellectual climate is against it. Most students find very little assistance, or even understanding, in their churches. The free reflection of the university gives them assurance that they can expose their fears, and also the hope that they can gain responsible and honest help.

7. One can believe that efforts to formulate the faith that deal with the real intellectual difficulties of the present, are in fact in the service of the church, even if the church lacks interest. In the long run, thoughtful and sensitive people will not stay in the church unless they believe that the church's message *can* make sense. The church needs those people.

8. Occasionally, the church recognizes its need for professional theological assistance. Sometimes it confronts a new topic, for example, ecology, where its existing rhetoric does not work. More obviously, the church needs, from time to time, to develop a new statement of faith. Then, too, it turns to its professionals for help.

It is not hard to see why Christian theologians are attracted to carrying out their vocations as university professionals. Life in the university is meaningful, secure, and satisfying for many. What they see happening in the church often does not attract them. They will serve when and as asked, but they find their major home in the university.

If the church is not much interested in what they do, they can seek respect in their professional guilds. They can find their rewards in the response of their students, especially those who go on to graduate school and commit themselves to carrying forward the discipline. If the church ignores them, they will largely ignore the church as well.

The Struggle to Respond

There are, of course, many theologians who have refused to accept the isolation from the church that academic professionalization engenders. They have divided their time between church and academy and built all kinds of bridges between them. This has often affected the way that they have taught their classes in theology. These efforts have mitigated the separation of theology from the church, but they have not prevented it.

The major challenge to professional academic theology has come from the liberation movements. There theology is closely related to the practical needs of the thinkers and the communities for which they speak. The fragmentation of theology into separate disciplines such as ethics makes no sense for them, nor does the traditional separation of theological and practical disciplines.

Within the academy the response to these theologies has been ambivalent. They are acknowledged as having some importance, and there is often an effort to include representatives of the ethnic groups for which they speak. Women, many of whom are feminists, have begun to play a central role in theological faculties. But, with a few interesting exceptions (such as Union Theological Seminary in New York and Drew University Theological School, Madison, New Jersey), neither ethnic spokespersons nor women have been allowed to reshape the curriculum or fundamentally change the definition of theology as a discipline. They function more to further pluralize what is taught. Partly through external pressures to conform to university norms, and partly because of the internalization of those norms, even feminist, black, Latin American, and other ethnic theologies become assimilated to disciplinary norms.

In any case, although these liberationist theologies sometimes show how pastors and lay people can become engaged in theological reflection, they do not immediately involve the dominant oldline community in doing its own theology. This community either takes a tolerant interest in what these groups do, or it becomes defensive toward them. Neither stance has yet led to serious theological reflection.

The professionalization of theologians and the transformation of theology into an academic discipline would not be so disturbing if ministers and lay Christians had found another way to reflect as Christians about the issues they face. The label *theology* is not the issue. But with the abandonment of theology by the church has gone the abandonment of intentional Christian thinking in general. This has gone so far that church leaders can hardly envision the formation of reflection groups within churches to consider the questions that face us. Some reflection about personal issues in light of Bible study is as far as most believe it is possible to go.

The renewal of the vocation of theology in the churches will not, and cannot, come from professional theologians whose work centers in academia. It can only come from the churches themselves, which, without such renewal, are condemned to continuing lukewarmness and the resulting decline. This does not mean that pastors and lay people in large numbers must study the writings of academic theologians. It does require that church people recognize that unless we reflect seriously, as Christians, about who we are and what we are called to be, we continue to drift into decadence. It also requires that, instead of being driven to despair by such recognition, we begin the process of reflection involving as many of our people as possible. As we of the church begin the process of our own reflection, we can be aided by some of the work done by professionals in responding to the challenges of our time.

The choice is not between maintaining ourselves by avoiding reflection and commitment on the one hand and losing members by reflecting and taking stands on the other. It is between losses caused by decadence and losses caused by faithfulness. If we continue as at present, the losses may be gradual, but there is no end in sight. If we commit ourselves to follow Christ as best we can, there is no guarantee of numerical growth. There is, however, a chance that the renewed authenticity will attract new people and become the basis for a new beginning.

2

Responding to the Loss of Cultural Props

Chapter 1 noted how the oldline churches have repented in face of new challenges posed to them in the twentieth century. It noted also that, though admirable, this has led to a state of confusion and lack of strong conviction. Assimilation of the new understanding into an inclusive and convincing formulation of Christian faith has not occurred. Indeed, this cannot occur without theological reflection, and the church has virtually abandoned theology. Chapter 1 also showed how the professionalization of the theologian and the "disciplinization" of theology led the church to abandon its calling to think about its faith and about the world in terms of its faith. It pointed to the need for the church to recognize that its abandonment of this calling is the deepest cause of its malaise. Only when this recognition occurs will the necessary efforts be made to recover the theological vocation.

Of course, we are not starting altogether from scratch in calling for theological reflection in the church. There has been some vigorous discussion about how the church should understand itself now and in the future. Two models have been proposed, both of them requiring for their achievement a reflective church. Both have emerged in response to what is perceived as a deep cultural historical transition—a time of endings and beginnings.

What is ending is often summed up in the phrase "the modern world," and this is useful. It is possible to identify, with little dispute, a number of features of this world that are dying. Here we will consider just three of these, along with two other endings whose beginnings antedate the modern world.

Endings

Eurocentrism

The first of these endings is that of Western hegemony, a period in which the main actors in world history have been the people of, or from, Western Europe. From the middle of the fifteenth century through the Second World War, the West was the determinative center of world affairs. In the latter part of this period, power passed into the hands of France, Germany, Great Britain, and the United States to such an extent that even Spain and Italy were marginalized.

A generation ago this had been true for so long, and it appeared so evident, that world histories were still written primarily from the perspective of the West. Ancient civilizations fed into Western Europe, and as Western Europe explored and expanded, other parts of the world were drawn into history. I will call this perspective *Eurocentrism,* recognizing that it treated even Eastern Europe only as contributory and derivative.

Eurocentrism dominated theology as well. The most influential American theologian of the previous generation, Reinhold Niebuhr, almost identified the history to whose interpretation he contributed so brilliantly, with that of the West. Alfred North Whitehead was only a little less parochial in his vision. But until the late sixties few noticed the distorting effects of this Eurocentrism in our most comprehensive thinkers.

Yet today, what was then taken for granted is widely recognized as problematic. There are still defenders of a Eurocentric reading of history and culture. But that it should need defense is a clear indication of the ending of an era. Many now view Western civilization as one among others, one whose hegemonic period is ending. Nor do we see this ending as something to be deplored. Viewed in a wider context, the evil involved in the dominance of the West is as striking as the good. As we remember Columbus' famous voyage, we no longer simply celebrate "our" discovery and settlement of the "new" world. We can also view the event and its consequences through the eyes of those who had discovered and settled these continents thousands of years earlier. We can mourn the destruction of their cultures, their people, and even their land.

Of course, Western power and influence remain great. One might even make the case that they have never been greater. The rival Eastern European block has capitulated and is ready to accept Western dominance. A United Europe will be the world's largest market. The world's only military "superpower" is Western.

Nevertheless, this does not contradict the earlier point. The unification of Europe results in part from competition with Asian economies, especially Japan. The military strength of the United States rests on a declining economic base that cannot sustain it indefinitely. Furthermore, ethnically and culturally, the United States has ceased to be simply Western; it is becoming pluralistic.

There is another counterargument to my thesis of the ending of Western hegemony. Many of the ideas and institutions originating in the West are now global. Indeed, the rise of such Asian powers as Japan would have been impossible apart from their adopting and adapting Western economic, technological, scientific, educational, and political institutions. Hence, it can be said that the West has won the war, and that all the powers that now contest the field are "Western."

There is some truth to this. What we witness is in part the global hegemony of Western culture as the completion of Western expansion and conquest. But this is not the whole story. The one area in which Western thought failed to win the victory throughout the whole period of its leadership was in religion and in those aspects of culture most closely tied to it. The church did establish itself in almost all countries, and in parts of the world where the dominant religions were primal, Christianity often competed with Islam in successful conversions. But where Christianity faced other axial traditions, such as Islam, Hinduism, and Buddhism, its advances were far more limited. This means that the hearts of most Asian cultures have never been captured by the West. They still beat to other rhythms. And in recent times these other rhythms have become remarkably attractive within Western Christendom as well. At the religious level, the main forms of Western Christianity—Protestantism and Roman Catholicism—are forced to view themselves as two among other forms of the religious spirit of humankind.

In addition, many of the most vital expressions of Christianity today are not in the West. In terms of active membership, a number of traditionally Western churches are now more African than European. Protestantism is more vigorous and expansionist in Korea than anywhere in the West. The Western churches are ceasing to be Western.

Hence, the church now operates in the context of the ending of Western hegemony. That involves a fundamental loss of confidence for many Western Christians. It means that what has been taken for granted as "progress" is no longer taking place or even self-evidently desirable. It means that the faith that once seemed obviously superior is now one tradition among others, seriously tainted by its long history of arrogance.

The global change has affected the internal situation in the United States. As long as Western Europe ruled the world, there was little question in the minds of most Americans that the United States was a Western nation. Africans, even when they were freed from slavery, were not considered a full part of the society. Immigrants from other countries in Europe, and from Asia and Latin America were welcome as workers, but if they were accepted as citizens at all, it was only as they were assimilated to the dominant Western culture. Creating American citizens in this sense out of the children of immigrants was a major mission of the public schools. The churches' missionary work with immigrants had much the same function. Church and government schools worked together to acculturate native Americans as well.

With the ending of Eurocentrism, the Europeanization of Asians, Latin Americans, Africans, and Native Americans has become problematic. Why should their cultures not be recognized? Why should the unity of the United States be attained by conformation to Western European standards? Pluralism has succeeded assimilation as the dominant ideal.

Nationalism and Economism

Inside the Western history that is now recognized as but one of several, other changes are occurring. One that is quite apparent, but still insufficiently noted, is a second ending, that of nationalism. It may seem untimely to speak of the ending of nationalism just when nationalisms are exploding so destructively in Eastern Europe. It must be emphasized that the ending has to do with Western Europe.

The most remarkable manifestation of the decline of nationalism is in Western Europe itself. Following the orgy of nationalism that was World War II, Western European countries have progressively subordinated their national sovereignty to transnational structures, especially to what was originally called the *European Economic Community*. Wars among Western European powers, which dominated global history for centuries, are now unthinkable.

If we ask what is replacing nationalism as the dominant force in European affairs, the answer is apparent. These affairs are driven quite explicitly by the quest for economic prosperity. It is for the sake of creating a larger market that European nations are subordinating their national interests. Nationalism has given way to "economism."

Although this is most apparent in Western Europe itself, it is true also of the United States government. The United States has subordinated its control of its own affairs to economic interests in developing the North American free trade zone with Canada and Mexico. It has gone further in a new General Agreement on Tariffs and Trade, which has created the World Trade Organization. In both of these agreements, the United States gives up some of its right to set its own standards on environment, agricultural subsidies, health, and working conditions when these standards adversely affect international trade.

Together with Western Europe and Japan, the United States has created a global market. This has been facilitated by the excessive borrowing of so many Third World countries in the 1970s, which has left them permanently indebted. Their financial difficulties have allowed the International Monetary Fund and the World Bank to impose structural adjustments on them that bind them permanently to international capital. Nationalist feeling may remain strong, but few Third World countries now have much control over their own affairs. Real nationalism is ended for them.

Even the great powers are increasingly governed by the global market. When Mitterand wanted to move France in a Socialist direction, the financial markets so assaulted the franc that he was forced to abandon his plans. The United States is not free to engage in policies that displease the currency traders.

Initially we exempted Eastern Europe from the thesis of the dying of nationalism. However, it has some relevance to what is happening there. The abandonment of communism by the Soviet Union was partly nationalistic, but it was also partly because prosperity seemed more important than national autonomy and power. Some of the independence movements in Eastern Europe expressed nationalisms that had been suppressed by the Soviet Empire, but some of them also reflected the belief that through independence from Russian hegemony, these countries could join the European market and share its prosperity.

The church is set in the context of these profound changes. Christians must decide whether they should make the same accommodations to the now triumphant economism that we long made to the previously dominant nationalism. Or does our faith require resistance to the commitment to economic growth at all costs? The debate about economism is raising the most serious theological issues now being discussed in our society. Should the church participate in that discussion?

Enlightenment Rationalism

In academic circles a third ending is talked about more than either of the preceding. This is the ending of rationalism, specifically the form of rationalism that came into dominance in the Enlightenment. This rationalism arose as a rejection of both the authority of antiquity and the speculative subtleties of the Scholastics, as well as an affirmation of the sufficiency of common sense as a guide to reality.

Of course, this rationalism is in fact far from dead. It still reigns supreme in many academic disciplines. Economism is based on it. Civil religion, also, continues to appeal to it. The churches' effort to do without theological reflection presupposes it.

Nevertheless, Enlightenment rationalism has been on the defensive for a long time. The great intellectuals have rejected it for more than a century. It is widely apparent that thought, and even perception, are far more radically conditioned by perspective and circumstance than rationalists supposed. Most people now recognize that what seems to be a matter of common sense in one culture does not appear as such in others. We no longer assume that people in other cultures are simply stupid and ignorant when what they see differs from what we see. We accept a relativistic stance with respect to many issues.

Problems with rationalism emerged two centuries ago within philosophy, and these problems have worked together with changing historical experience to undermine its power in the general public. But decisive for its demise was its collapse within physics. This is because it was the success that followed the adoption of rationalism by physics that gave it such great prestige. When physicists discovered that what they took to be the only possible rational concepts were not applicable to the building blocks of nature, this support of rationalism was withdrawn. Physicists no longer suppose that their categories can provide a unified and coherent view of reality. Even if they could develop a unified mathematical theory, it would make little contact with any ideas available to common sense. And the great majority of them are prepared to live indefinitely with incoherence as long as they can continue to predict and control. The failure of rationalism in physics undercuts the conviction that it is adequate in other spheres.

The collapse of rationalism in physics also undercut the Enlightenment worldview. That worldview was mechanistic, treating all nature as a set of machines. This involved determinism—the assumption that when initial conditions in a closed system are set, the operation of that system is forever determined.

The Enlightenment worldview vacillated between including human beings in this deterministic, mechanistic system, and viewing them dualistically as of a metaphysically different order. For most practical purposes the latter view has dominated, even when theoretically it has been acknowledged that human beings are part of nature. This dominance has been associated with an anthropocentrism that has treated human beings as the only locus of intrinsic value. Any value attributed to other things has been their instrumental value for human beings.

Both the units of nature and human beings have been understood substantialistically and individualistically. Substances are thought of as the kinds of things that have independent existence and whose fundamental nature can be identified without reference to other things. Hence, individuals exist first as what they are in and by themselves, and only incidentally enter into relations with others.

The Christianity we have inherited, especially in Protestant circles, is one that adapted itself extensively to Enlightenment rationalism and the associated worldview. Its ideas about God have been based on a rational understanding of the Creator of an orderly world. Sometimes this God is seen as the cause of the general laws that operate in the world in a way that leaves some room for human freedom, with moral law taking up where physical laws leave off. Sometimes God is viewed as the ground of a fully deterministic order. Some hold that God can violate the laws of nature in miraculous acts. Others see no place for intervention when the laws themselves are God's perfect work. Heated debates have raged over alternatives such as these. But the collapse of Enlightenment rationalism cuts the ground from under all of these still popular ideas.

The church must live and work in a world in which most of the ideas that have supported faith in God in the past have been rejected. This is widely known, even when the knowledge is resisted. It leads to a deepening divide between those who dogmatically and militantly reaffirm beliefs in which they no longer have rational confidence and those who have become skeptical, even cynical, about any sort of theistic claim.

Sexual Revolution

A fourth ending inside the West is currently being felt in the churches with greater intensity. It is the ending of the long epoch of sexual repression. This sexual repression has been closely connected with Christianity, even though its origins are not biblical.

The sexual repression reached its cultural culmination about a century ago. This was accompanied by a reaction that initiated the sexual revolution. That revolution has been amazingly successful in opening up public discourse about sexual topics. Combined with contraceptives, the revolution has also led to a great deal of freedom in sexual practice, beginning in adolescence and even earlier. It has made all our sexual institutions, even the family, problematic.

In the past fifty years, the sexual revolution, originally directed *against* the churches, has made great inroads *within* them. Almost no one now avowedly affirms that sex is something unclean or evil to be minimized as much as possible. Among Roman Catholics there is no longer any self-evident spiritual superiority of the celibate life, and hence there is greatly diminished willingness to adopt it for the sake of priestly ministry.

Nevertheless, although few defend the agelong advocacy of sexual repression, that repression is our Christian legacy. Most Christians still support institutions and rules that were connected with it. These are still thought of as Christian morality, and many, even some who do not live by this morality themselves, want the church to continue to sanction it. This commitment to inherited patterns is clearly demonstrated by the intense condemnation of homosexuality. The dominant situation at present is, on the one hand, the affirmation of the goodness of sexuality and, on the other hand, its restriction to legal marriage, which is not available to all. This generates both resentment and confusion. It is in the context of this confusion that we must think through the Christian understanding of sexuality.

Eurocentrism, nationalism, and Enlightenment rationalism with its accompanying worldview are all features of modernity. Hence, their ending indicates the end of the modern era. But what has ended because of the sexual revolution occurred long before modernity. This is even more true of another ending, the beginning of which we may now be witnessing: the ending of patriarchy.

Patriarchy

The ending of many of the features of our heritage discussed above is far advanced. If we are indeed witnessing the beginning of the end of patriarchy, we must recognize that it is just the beginning. Yet we can say with confidence that some of the more blatant features of patriarchy are ending and that, at quite deep levels, what was until very recently self-evident has been called into question.

For example, it is no longer self-evident that the institution of marriage should continue at all. Even assuming that heterosexual couples *should* continue to be, along with their young children, basic units of society, it is no longer clear that men and women should play distinctive roles in this partnership. It is no longer clear which of our images of male and female are socially constructed and which can and should be changed. It is no longer clear whether women have distinctive contributions to make to a new society, or whether, with the change of gender roles, there will be little distinction between their contributions and those of men.

One reason for grave hesitation in declaring the ending of patriarchy is that the changes involved are unimaginably great. Probably all the other endings I have mentioned are included within the ending of patriarchy, but it extends far beyond them. We have no real difficulty in imagining a non-Eurocentric world or a society in which sex is not repressed. Such societies have existed in the past, and they are far advanced in the present. But we have acute difficulty in imagining a nonpatriarchal society. We are not sure whether one has ever existed, and presently we have only fragmentary anticipations.

Even the fragmentary anticipations that are present in today's society are exceedingly disturbing to many. Without established gender roles, many men, and indeed many women as well, are fundamentally unclear about who they are and how to relate to one another. It seems that male violence against women, expressing anger against their threat to male self-understanding, is on the rise. How far patriarchal self-understanding can be overcome without a much greater, and possibly victorious, backlash cannot be determined. If the family as such is a patriarchal institution, it is quite unclear what new structure can replace it or whether society can survive at all without this basic structure.

These comments should be taken simply as an expression of the current confusion and uncertainty and not as predictions. What can be said with some confidence, however, is that the church finds itself in a culture that is confused about gender roles and unsure about institutions and personal habits that have been taken for granted for thousands of years. These perplexities will deepen over the years with profound consequences for the church.

During a time of endings, one common response is to seek refuge in old "verities." Some turn to the church, expecting it to reaffirm the beliefs and practices of the past. The pressures on the church today are conservative and even reactionary.

When people are hurting and confused, there is an important place for personal support and reassurance. The church in every age serves as this source of comfort. But this is not an adequate response if it includes reaffirmation of teachings that lack Christian warrant and are damaging to others or to those who hold them. The mission of the church in the years ahead must be more than agreeing with those who want to create an island of unchanging certainties in a context of flux.

Proposals for Reforming the Church

Renewal

There are, on the other hand, two quite serious and valid proposals for reforming the church in this time of endings. The first is to concentrate on the inner life of the church, especially on the local congregation. If we recognize that during the modern period the church accommodated itself much too fully to modern cultural trends, we can now learn the error of such cultural accommodation in general. Our task as Christians, then, is not to adapt ourselves to what is going on in the society around us, but to be faithful to Jesus Christ.

Further, we now recognize that in the past we have made claims to universality that have led us to betray Christ in our arrogance and imperialism. Acknowledging this, we can now learn to concentrate on our own commitments without seeking to impose them on others. Our task as Christians is to be true disciples and to constitute ourselves as true communities. If we recognize that we have formulated our beliefs in categories borrowed from others, we can now learn to trust the language of our own heritage without trying to impose this on all. The task is to live into, and to be shaped by, the symbols of our faith. I will call this form of church life "renewal."

Those who advocate renewal understand very well what is involved in the ending of modernity. They disconnect authentic Christian faith from its close connection to European culture and accept the end of its dominance. They understand deeply that authentic Christianity has always been in tension with nationalism, and they call for fuller purification of the church from this distortion. They see in the ending of rationalism a great opportunity for the church to reaffirm its own distinctive vision without supposing that it must justify it in a wider context that is thought to have superior knowledge.

The relation of the renewal model to the sexual revolution and the feminist attack on patriarchy is less positive. It appreciates liberating our reading of the Bible from the antisexual hermeneutic that has dominated it for so long. But what we find in the Bible is an attitude toward sexuality very different from that of the sexual revolution. It is the biblical view, and not our dominant cultural view, that renewal affirms.

The tension with current developments is even clearer with respect to patriarchy. Advocates of renewal, in the name of biblical teaching, affirm justice for all, and this certainly includes women. Hence they support many of the gains for women that have been realized through feminist leadership, but they do not support the wholesale attack on patriarchy. They appreciate the positive elements in feminism from a biblical point of view, but they do not accept criticism of the Bible from a feminist perspective.

Transformation

The second valid proposal for reform of the church today understands Christianity somewhat differently. This reform proposal views Christianity as a movement that lives always out of its past but in such a way that it learns from and is changed by its cultural environment, while also taking responsibility to Christianize that environment. From the collapse of modernity, the lesson it draws is not that Christianity should have kept itself pure and unaffected by modernity, but that it accommodated itself uncritically and did too little to affect the shape that modernity took.

In this view, our task as Christians is not to recover an original form of life in the church. That form was a creative response to the circumstances of that time. It was shaped out of its past in sensitive interaction with the particularities of its environment. Our task, as we try faithfully to continue the Christian tradition, is to respond as effectively and appropriately today to the particularities of our situation as the early church responded in its time. That may involve reproducing some of its teachings and practices, but that is not the main thing. Our task is to be transformed by the best of what we are now experiencing and learning and to share in the transformation of the world. Instead of concentrating on the deepening socialization of those within the church into inherited images and rituals, it concentrates on reaching out to those who have been alienated from the church by the incredibility and oppressiveness of many of its teachings. I will call this model of reform "transformation."

The advocates of transformation respond to the ending of modernity in ways that are similar to, but also different from, the advocates of renewal. They are committed to being transformed by the ending of Eurocentrism, to repent of the long enslavement of Christianity to European culture. But they may affirm some elements of that culture as lasting contributions to the healthy development of Christianity.

Like renewalists they are committed to freeing themselves from the dying nationalism, but their response to the ending of rationalism is somewhat different. Whereas renewal sees this as an opportunity to reaffirm traditional symbols and meaning without justifying or commending them to a wider culture, transformation sees the dying of common sense Enlightenment rationalism as an occasion for renewing a more radical intellectual questioning. The ending of the hegemony of the Enlightenment worldview opens the way for Christians to help shape a new and better one.

The differences are clearest in the responses to the sexual revolution and feminism. Whereas renewal views them from the perspective of biblical teaching, transformation assumes that we now have knowledge about sexuality and gender that was not available to biblical authors. Our teaching and practice should be transformed by this knowledge. That does not mean that we accept everything that the leaders of the sexual revolution or of feminism say. But it does mean that we interact with them for the purpose of learning what we cannot learn from the Bible, and that we take the new insights seriously in the reworking of our theory and practice.

Beginnings

The account of the situation thus far has emphasized what is ending rather than what is coming into being, although the latter was not excluded. The endings are clearer than the beginnings. Just what is coming into being is not yet determined, but we cannot afford to be indifferent. What takes the place of what is dying is of great importance for our children and for their children after them. We can and should project possibilities, if not certainties, and propose appropriate alliances and directions.

1. The ending of Eurocentrism can mean the beginning of a wide dispersal of power, especially the power of self-determination. It is not possible to say that this is now happening globally. Indeed, because the economy is under the control of fewer and fewer people, the opposite is occurring. Yet there are countervailing forces. Long silent people are announcing their refusal to continue to be mere objects of history, and some of them are finding ways to embody their new demands for participation. The pluralistic ideal is widely accepted, at least rhetorically. But there remains the question of what a truly pluralistic society can be like. What can unify it other than a dying nationalism or the values of one or another of its subcultures?

For churches in this country, the movement toward acceptance of those who have long been excluded from power, even from membership, is far advanced. Even at the local level much is happening. At the denominational level, the ending of Eurocentrism has given visibility and status to persons of color. In the World Council of Churches much of the leadership is passing to people in the Third World. Of all the changes involved in the previously mentioned endings, this one is furthest advanced.

The end of Eurocentrism has not only introduced ethnic pluralism as a new ideal and practice within the church but has also changed the church's relation to other religious communities. Formerly, this relationship was one of competition, with conversion of adherents of the other tradition being the goal. Now dialogue has become widespread. Dialogue need not lack an element of traditional concern. In serious dialogue, one tries to persuade, but dialogue presupposes mutual respect and willingness to take seriously the other's efforts to persuade as well. That was not a central part of the earlier mission.

2. The end of nationalism and the current triumph of economism are highly ambiguous. Nationalism came into being partly to overcome the fratricidal consequences of religious animosities in the first half of the seventeenth century, established a modus vivendi among neighbors with differing faiths, and embodied communal feelings of a healthy kind. All this is threatened by the dominance of economism.

On the other hand, nationalism too often claimed for the nation state an absolute loyalty of which it is wholly unworthy. Even when it did not go that far, it absorbed idealistic commitments of its citizens into support for policies that were inimical to other peoples. In all-too-common extreme cases, it expressed itself in colonialism and imperialism. Having put an end to internal religious wars, it only increased the number of wars among nations, leading to the climactic horrors of the two world wars.

The economism that has replaced nationalism has greatly reduced the threat of major wars, especially now that the Eastern block has ceased to function as an opposing economistic ideology. This is an enormous accomplishment. Economism at its best is devoted to the economic welfare of all peoples as it understands that welfare. And in certain parts of the world it has greatly reduced poverty.

But the absolutization of economic growth as a goal justifies the supposedly temporary imposition of enormous suffering on the poor and even on the middle class. Economism increases the wealth and the power of the few, while widening the gap between these and others. And it makes it more and more difficult for the great majority of people to influence the conditions of their own existence. Finally, it speeds up the exploitation of the earth's resources and hastens the day of the collapse of the biosphere.

This threat to the earth has evoked a strong reaction. Defense of the earth has become a rallying cry for millions and has elicited deep commitment from tens of thousands. Earthism is emerging as a powerful spiritual alternative to economism.

The chief problem with earthism is that it sometimes distracts attention from commitment to justice for the poor and oppressed. Its critics often give support to economism in their insistence that the economic needs of the poor must have priority over preservation of the natural world. But there are signs that earthism is getting beyond that dilemma. As it becomes clearer that the economics of economism impoverishes the poor, mutual suspicion between environmentalists and the poor is giving way to recognition of shared concerns. Christians are helping to envision a different economics, one that takes the earth seriously. This form of economics can and will also keep central the meeting of basic human needs and the empowering of the poor and oppressed to take responsibility for their own lives and communities.

3. The end of Enlightenment rationalism has meant primarily the rejection of all efforts to make coherent sense of the world. It has supported the fragmentation of knowledge into autonomous academic disciplines and the silencing of questions of value and meaning. In physics it has meant the acceptance of procedures that work despite the incoherence of the concepts associated with them. It can take the form of direct denial of any connection between thought or language and some other reality, such as the natural world or human experience. Language is sometimes depicted as the inclusive horizon of what is.

There is, however, an alternative response to the end of Enlightenment rationalism and its accompanying worldview. This is a renewal of the speculative intellectual effort to probe behind cultural common sense to more radical modes of thought, and behind the surface of things to deeper realities. This is a quest for a new way of thinking about reality. The recognition that every theory is conditioned by the perspective of the thinker can be deeply internalized without the rejection of theoretical work or the denial that some theories are better than others. This alternative response is giving rise to a more organic, ecological, relational, communal, nondualist, nonsubstantialist, and nonanthropocentric way of thinking of human beings and their world.

4. The sexual revolution has been profoundly liberating, freeing many people from internal repression and external oppression. It has allowed them to find more personal fulfillment in their relations with others. It has also brought new forms of suffering in its wake. Sexual liberation has introduced new forms of sexual exploitation. Also, it has led many to posit sexual fulfillment as the central element in hu-

man fulfillment. It has undercut an emphasis on personal commitment and mutual faithfulness and willingness to make personal sacrifices for the sake of community. It has contributed to a situation in which more children grow up without a healthy homelife.

These problems are generating a backlash in favor of traditional teachings about sexual morality. Yet few are attempting to reintroduce the negative attitudes toward sexuality that were so long associated with these teachings. Youth receive profoundly mixed messages from their elders, and the great majority see no reason to restrict sexual intercourse to marriage. Most married couples see no reason to continue marriages that are no longer satisfying, sexually or otherwise.

Advocates of the sexual revolution believe that many of the continuing problems would be solved if society unambiguously affirmed the centrality of sexuality in human life and ordered itself so as to enable each individual to attain maximum sexual satisfaction. They see no inherent advantage in channeling sexual activity exclusively into long-term committed relations. They object to subordinating the quest for sexual satisfaction to other aspects of human relationships. To project their vision of society into the future is to imagine a situation quite different from any that has existed in the past.

5. Feminism arose in part out of the realization that the liberation at which the sexual revolution aimed was too often the freedom of males to exploit females. What women want and need from sex may not be identical with what many males desire. But the feminist movement has gone far beyond this resistance to male interpretations of sexual liberation.

Feminists have carried the critique of our society and of our Christian tradition to new depths. Although their greatest strength has been the exposure of injustice and distortion based on power imbalance, they have also pointed toward directions that we can now take in the church and in the wider society that gradually will bring a more just and honest society into being. Their thinking remains dynamic, with new criticisms and fresh insights continuously assailing those who will listen. No one knows just where this will lead, but in many respects the directions are clear and radical.

Feminists call for changes in power relations and in the basic conception of power itself. Power should no longer be viewed only as control of others but rather as empowerment. Feminists want gender roles to become much more fluid and reject much traditional rhetoric, showing how it presupposes and supports deep-seated patri-archal assumptions. They strongly affirm sexual pleasure, but they generally see it more as part of human relations. Their focus is on the quality of these relations rather than on regulating when and where sexual acts should be approved.

Christian feminists lead in the study of the Bible. They both dis-play its dominant patriarchal character and retrieve subordinate non-patriarchal themes. For them the dominance of the former cannot mean its authority for the present. What is subordinate in scripture, even more in tradition, must become normative for future Christians.

Response to the Beginnings

We can now flesh out the account of renewal and transformation in relation to these comments about the beginnings that accompany the endings.

1. Both renewal and transformation are receptive to some post-modern developments following on the dying of Eurocentrism. Both affirm ethnic pluralism, for example. Yet even here they differ. Re-newal calls for a faithful church that repents and eschews all racial and cultural arrogance and prejudice and undertakes to embody in its own life its ideal of inclusivism. Transformation calls both for this and for leadership in helping society as a whole to find a convincing image of pluralism and then to embody this in its actual life. The empowerment of diverse peoples is, for the advocates of transformation, a goal to be directly pursued in the world as well as within the life of the church.

The differences are more marked with respect to dialogue with persons representing other religious traditions. For renewal this is not a high priority. Indeed, there is some skepticism that persons from di-verse communities of religious thought and practice can truly under-stand one another at all. Each linguistic system is different, renewal af-firms, and the terms do not have a common referent outside the system.

Transformation, on the other hand, sees the possibility of interact-ing with persons who have a different religious experience and who have gained a different wisdom as a great opportunity. To learn from them can mean both enrichment and transformation of Christian un-derstanding. Dialogue is also a context in which the gospel can be shared without arrogance and pressure.

2. Both renewal and transformation not only reject the dying nationalism but also oppose the economism that is taking its place. Nationalism and economism are idolatries to which Christians cannot subscribe without distortion of their faith. But in their attitudes to earthism they differ.

Renewal emphasizes that earthism, too, is an idolatry that is to be rejected. That does not mean that concern for the earth is wrong, any more than love of one's country or concern for meeting economic needs of all people are wrong. But it does mean that care for the earth has a subordinate place in an overall renewal of the biblical vision.

Transformation, on the other hand, while recognizing the danger of idolatry in every "ism," is seeking allies in its quest for radical change in the direction of public policies that threaten the very possibility of a decent future for life on this planet. Transformation welcomes earthism as an ally in this project, and it gives earthism what support it can.

3. Renewal and transformation differ in their views of what should follow the dying of Enlightenment rationalism. Renewal emphasizes that the collapse of a universal rationality frees Christians to assert our own vision and values without the pressure to justify them before a supposedly superior tribunal. It emphasizes the relativistic implications of the new situation. This entails the rejection of the earlier Christian habit of trying to impose Christian beliefs and practices on others.

Transformation sees a great opportunity for the church to ally itself with aspects of the emerging constructive postmodern worldview and to take part in shaping it. It sees a real chance of the widespread emergence of a postmodern culture that is far more congenial to Christian beliefs. It may also be possible to help shape this culture in such a way that it will support the new directions so urgently needed in public policy. This interest in a positive worldview assumes that while no beliefs are final or free from the influence of particularities of context, some are truly better than others, and that it is eminently worthwhile to support the better and oppose the worse.

4. Most of what can be said about the respective responses to the sexual revolution has already been said. Both renewal and transformation accept the fundamental goodness of sexuality. Neither accepts all the ideas that advocates of the sexual revolution put forth. Yet it is worthwhile to spell out their differences more specifically. Indeed,

this is especially important because the most heated discussion in the church today is over sexual morality.

Renewal aims to develop a biblical sexual morality. This will affirm the goodness of sexuality as a gift of God, but it will emphasize that it is given for particular purposes. Its use and enjoyment outside the appropriate contexts is condemned. Since such references as are made to homosexuality in the Bible are negative, a biblical sexual morality today will condemn homosexual practice.

Transformation agrees that sexuality is a gift of God and that it should be used responsibly. However, it does not take the attitudes of biblical writers as definitive with respect to what such responsible use and enjoyment should be. It assumes that their teachings were relevant to their situation and their knowledge. Our situation is different, and much more is known about sexuality today. To address the new situation and to assimilate the knowledge now available requires the criticism of some biblical teachings and the transformation of received Christian doctrine and practice. For those committed to transformation, to condemn those who are attracted only to persons of their own gender to lifelong sexual asceticism is contrary to what Christ now calls us to do and be.

5. Differences with respect to feminism are similar. Renewal views feminist ideas from a biblical perspective. This enables it to affirm some of them. For example, it may be reminded by feminists that the church has too often subscribed to views of power, and to practices based on them, that are not supported by the Bible. The Bible emphasizes that the exercise of power is for the sake of the weak, not the strong, so that it condemns all expressions of patriarchalism in which men use their power for their own aggrandizement.

But renewal opposes the wholesale challenge to biblical authority entailed in the rejection of biblical patriarchalism, the effort to replace many of the basic symbols and images of the Christian community, the questioning of the ideal of servanthood at least in its application to women, and the call for revolutionary changes in the relations of males and females. These appear to entail a subordination of biblical authority to that of a contemporary ideological movement. This is sharply opposed to the whole aim of renewal.

Transformation, on the other hand, views feminism, at least in some of its Christian forms, as a major ally for the transformation of the church and the world. This can never mean that every position adopted by every feminist is accepted. That would be absurd, since there are important disagreements among feminists themselves. But the ferment of radical, critical thought, and the efforts to envision how this can be played out in the world, are just what transformation is all about.

One caveat is needed. There are Christian feminists for whom feminist identity is primary, and Christian identity, secondary. They do not embody the transformation model, however rich their contributions to transformation may be. The transformation model is one in which Christian identity is primary. But this Christian identity is understood to require openness to wisdom wherever it is found and readiness to be transformed by it. Advocates of transformation find much of the most important wisdom today to be offered by feminists.

Two Moments in a Single Process

Renewal and transformation are not to be viewed as opposites. They are two images of an alternative to the current drift and lukewarmness of the oldline churches. They resemble one another more than they differ. On many issues—for example, in their opposition to institutionalism, their insistence that Christians should form their lives wholly by their faith rather than in compromise with the world, and their condemnation of the idolatries that so pervasively afflict our culture—they are allies.

They differ, but even in their difference there are ironies. Renewal is by far the more common explicit theme in scripture and tradition. Again and again prophets and reformers have called for recovery of past forms of faith against the compromises of the present. Yet again and again the result has been more like what is called for by transformation.

One may therefore think of renewal and transformation as two moments in a single process. Paul called on us to be transformed by the renewing of our minds. Both individually and institutionally, there is no transformation without renewal, and renewal inevitably transforms.

Neither is unproblematic. Like all personal and historical events, there are ambiguities. The excesses of each call for the other. Consider the history of the Western church in broad outlines.

The early church found itself in a Hellenistic world. It condemned much in that world as idolatrous and superstitious, but there was also much in it that was attractive to eyes formed by the biblical faith. Greek philosophers had answered genuine questions that biblical authors had not even posed. There was real wisdom there. Christians must choose between closing themselves to that wisdom so as to maintain the purity of their faith or appropriate and modify it from the perspective of their faith. The church as a whole chose the latter. It transformed Greek philosophy, and it was transformed by it.

This process culminated with Augustine and Thomas Aquinas. They provided, and still provide for many, a way to incorporate all thought and experience into a unified, distinctively Christian, whole. They have made possible the wholehearted faith apart from which the church relapses into lukewarmness.

But the church paid a price for this transformation. Although it faithfully carried forward much of its biblical heritage, it also neglected other elements in the process of incorporating Greek wisdom. There was always the danger that instead of appropriating philosophy from a biblical perspective, the Bible would be read through the eyes of the philosophy. This danger was accentuated as tradition came to mediate scripture with little chance for scripture to critique tradition.

Reaction to these distortions led to calls for renewal, culminating in Luther and Calvin. Reform required purifying the church of elements that were not warranted by biblical authority and recovering elements of biblical thought that had been obscured. The result was a transformation of the church and its teaching rather than an actual reenactment of any earlier form. It was hardly less selective in its appropriation of scripture than the earlier transformationists had been. It continued much that had been borrowed from Greek and Roman cultures, and it expressed the current influence of the cultures of northern Europe. Also, it was informed by new elements in the culture of the time, especially the humanistic scholarship.

Nevertheless, it was as clear an instance of renewal as history offers. It *intended* faithfulness to scripture, and this intention deeply affected its decisions about the new institutions it created and the doctrines it formulated. Although it did not exclude elements that came from extracanonical sources, it did not systematize these or seek a synthesis between them and the biblical teaching. Although *sola scriptura* exaggerates, it rightly points to the insistence on justifying each decision from the Bible in a relatively direct way.

Renewal here is not an attempt to repeat unchanged any past form of Christianity or church life. The attempt is to recover the pure stream of biblical teaching from its mixture with other sources and to act on that alone. There have been some advocates of renewal who went further in seeking to model the life of the church on that of the earliest congregations, but in general the meaning of renewal in subsequent Protestantism has followed that of the Reformers.

Neither renewal nor transformation can be a once-for-all matter. The results of either tend to become rigidified and transmitted as if this were so. The Roman Catholic Church gave peculiar authority to the Thomistic synthesis in such a way as to resist new forms of wisdom in the surrounding culture and in other cultures. In the twentieth century Pope John XXIII led the church in a new transformation through the remarkable Second Vatican Council. Once again the doors were thrown open to the selective appropriation of what other communities and traditions could offer.

Lutheran and Calvinist churches have alternated between two ways of being faithful to their founders. On the one side is an emphasis on the particular doctrines through which their founders recovered biblical themes that had been obscured in the medieval synthesis. On the other side is an open-ended continuing study of scripture that sometimes leads to results that are in tension with the Reformers. Just as the Catholic Church turned the radical openness and inclusiveness of Thomas into a principle of closure and exclusiveness, so many Protestants have exchanged the genuine search of the Scriptures into a defense of particular confessional statements summarizing the findings of sixteenth-century scholars. Renewal today aims to build on our best current knowledge of scripture rather than on past orthodoxies.

This historical overview has depicted transformation and renewal as the distinctive styles of Catholic and Protestant Christianity, respectively. There is some justification for this. Catholics in general do aim at inclusiveness and that leads in principle to openness to all sources of knowledge. They are committed to a unifying Christian vision. The term "protestant" rightly suggests a greater emphasis on critique rather than on synthetic thinking, on the avoidance of error rather than on the appropriation of all wisdom. But there have been many movements of renewal in Catholicism and many efforts at transformation among Protestants.

Whereas the early church's greatest intellectual challenge was

Greek philosophy, the greatest challenge facing Christianity in the early modern period was natural science. Since a major obstacle to appropriating the new science was the continuing power of Aristotelian thought, the rejection of Aristotle's authority by the Reformers gave a certain advantage to Protestants. Although some Protestants have insisted that knowledge of the natural world is to be gleaned only from the Bible, most have wanted to give natural scientists freedom and have taken the results of their work seriously. This led to an appropriation of science and its worldview by many Protestants analogous to the appropriation of Platonic and Aristotelian thinking by the early and medieval church.

Sociologically speaking, this was the closest approximation to transformation in Protestant history prior to the nineteenth century. Unfortunately, this appropriation of natural science, especially during the eighteenth century, was far less critical than the appropriation of Greek thought had been. Hence this Protestant "transformation" is a poorer example than either of the Catholic ones mentioned above. The result was a mixture of biblical and Enlightenment thinking in which the worldview associated with modern science was often dominant. There were individual theologians who wrestled responsibly with the issues involved, but on the whole, Protestant theologians retreated before the sciences rather than creatively transforming their thought through critical appropriation of scientific knowledge. Only when controversy over evolution forced the church to engage scientific thought directly did transformationist modes of thought assume some importance in relation to the natural sciences.

Although Luther and Calvin saw the Bible as providing a comprehensive orientation to life, society, and nature, many of their renewalist followers have found it necessary to draw boundaries. Much of the most creative work of Protestant thinkers has been in establishing the discrete areas in which science and theology operate. They provide a way of accepting both, which does not require the transformation of either.

In the nineteenth century, Protestant theology faced a different challenge to which its response has been far more critical and genuinely transformative. This challenge was the rise of historical consciousness. Since Protestantism began as a movement of renewal based on a style of interpretation of scripture learned from humanists, it was inherently open to historical questioning. Protestant scholars led in the development of the historical consciousness. Nevertheless, this took on a life of its own and forced difficult responses from the church. These responses involved conscious transformation of the way in which the Bible and its relation to us are understood. A large segment of the Christian community has been carried through this transformation and now reads the Bible historically. Renewal as described above is one of the products of the profound transformation of Protestantism effected by the historical consciousness.

Advocates of renewal sometimes polemicize against transformation, and advocates of transformation often give only a small place to renewal. Nevertheless, in broad historical perspective it seems that both have roles to play in the life of the church. When the problem is that the distinctive biblical themes are clouded by the dominance of cultural patterns, renewal is needed. Transformation is needed when our historic teaching limits us to the themes dominant in our own tradition, preventing us from hearing the voices of those who have suffered, because of our historic teaching, and when this limitation blocks our appropriation of liberating and enlarging insights from other sources. Our historical consciousness should prevent us from supposing that we can make normative judgments applicable to all places and all times.

If we ask which direction we should take today, the answer will be shaped by our judgment of the present situation. If we judge that our greatest problem is that our churches have become reflective of the general culture and that our people no longer know what it means to be distinctively Christian, then renewal is likely to suggest itself as the most appropriate response. The church cannot effectively engage in transformation, either of itself or of the world, if its members do not know who they are as Christians.

On the other hand, we may judge that the changes going on in our world make past forms of Christianity unsuitable and that the potential contribution of Christianity to believers and to the world alike can be realized only through repentance for what we have been. In that case, despite all difficulties, we must try to proceed with the transformations whose partial execution has left us in the present dispirited condition. This will require thoughtful and selective retrieval of elements in our past that have been obscured and a much more critical stance toward dominant forces in the culture. But these steps will emphasize open interaction with the culture all the same.

There can be neither renewal nor transformation without widespread theological reflection. Renewal is far from a simple matter of looking up proof texts and applying them. It does not suppose that there can be repetition today of any past form of the church. It does not claim to find in the Bible a ready-made pattern of symbols into which Christians can now be socialized. On the contrary, entering into the Christian symbolic system and enacting it well requires extensive reflection.

Transformation is even more demanding in this regard. It requires reflection not only about the retrieval of elements in the tradition, but also about what is found in the culture around us. To be critical of the culture requires more reflection than to disconnect from it. And to appropriate some elements from that culture that differ from what we retrieve from our own tradition also requires fresh theological reflection.

Hence, whether we choose the way of renewal or the way of transformation, we confront the same difficulty noted as the cause of our malaise. The church has lost the ability to think. Unless it recognizes that its healthy survival depends on the recovery and exercise of that ability and acts on that recognition, talk of either renewal or transformation is idle.

3

Seeing God at Work
in Transformation

Although both renewal and transformation are needed in church history, transformation has a certain priority. It is, first, the more inclusive ideal, and the argument will be made that it includes elements lacking in renewal that are needed in the church at least some of the time. The further argument will be that these elements are particularly important today. This chapter will conclude with a transformationist proposal for the oldline church.

Within scripture one finds the note of renewal frequently. The prophets looked back to a time when the people of Israel were more faithful and called them back to that time. Later Jews hoped for the restoration of the Davidic monarchy in all its glory.

Nevertheless, what is more distinctive of the Jewish and Christian scriptures, especially in comparison with those of other communities, is their emphasis on what is to be. This is rarely depicted as a renewal of what has been, the pre-fallen state, for example, though in later tradition this identification sometimes occurs. In Jesus' message the kingdom of God is something new that can be expected. What is to be is different from, and much more than, what was.

This is by no means denied by the advocates of renewal. They want to renew the expectancy that characterizes the New Testament writings, the living toward and from the future. But there is a paradox here. In the early church that expectancy was associated with new modes of experience, adventurous action, and the development of novel ways of thinking. The only canon was the Jewish scripture, and the new Christian writings went far beyond simple retrieval of elements from that canon. If we try to retrieve this expectancy while limiting the style of church life to what is derived from the congealed results of that radical freedom and novelty, it will not be a genuine retrieval. A true retrieval of future-orientation will give us in our time something of the freedom and courage to think and act in new ways that characterized the early church. It is highly unlikely that our transformation of Christianity will be as radical as was their transformation of Judaism, but it can share in the transforming spirit and activity.

This transforming character of genuine openness to the future in the early church is a special case of the process through which the whole canon came into being. The Judaism of the Second Temple was different from the Judaism of the First Temple. The faith of the prophets was different from that of the patriarchs. The study of the Jewish scriptures shows how Hebrew understanding changed and developed and how at any given time it was diverse. Furthermore, it shows that much of this change and development and diversity resulted from interaction with other religious cultures. This does not mean that Jewish faith was syncretistic. The Jews adapted what they adopted, and they integrated it into an ongoing tradition. Even when they canonized some body of literature, the living tradition continued to appropriate from others without loss of its own identity.

In short the Jewish canon—what we call the Old Testament—is the precipitate of a long process of creative transformations of Hebrew faith. We can discern common themes and even speak of a theology of the Old Testament, but a deeper study is likely to locate God in the process of transmitting traditions in ever-changing forms. It is a mistake to treat the canonized materials as providing a fixed symbolic system into which we can be socialized.

That does not mean that we should oppose socialization into the community that lives from and in the history whose formative period is recorded in that canon. Quite the contrary. But to be socialized into that community is to be socialized into a community that did not cease to be creatively transformed once the canon was closed. For the church to learn and grow in interaction with the Greeks, Romans, and Germans, and now with the Muslims, Hindus, and Buddhists, is to continue the process we discern in the canon, of the Hebrews learning through interaction with Canaanites, Egyptians, Babylonians, Persians, and Greeks.

Christians sometimes argue that this dynamic history of transformation ended with Jesus Christ. In him, it is said, we have finality and completeness, so that once the meaning of this event was settled by the church no further transformation has been desirable. Change after the kerygma was proclaimed, the canon closed, or the creeds fixed is heresy. For those who think in this way, renewal is indeed the correct response. Although there may be room for continuing interpretation and reformulation for the sake of intelligibility in different cultural contexts, there is nothing of relevance to be learned from other sources.

Rudolf Bultmann's theology has something of this character. The Old Testament in his estimation tells a story of a failed quest. The proclamation of the meaning of Jesus' death by his disciples provides the one key to the authentic life of faith. For Christians the theological task since then has been to point to that message and display its power to save in all times and places. There can be no further development.

This position was possible only through an existential interpretation of eschatology. To adopt it we must withdraw attention from the temporal futurity of the Kingdom, for example, and ask only about its presence to each person in each moment, as a call to a way of being that is open to the future. Further, this openness to the future is a universal possibility not affected in principle by the particularity of the historical context. Thus history ends in Jesus.

This solution to the theological problematic had great relevance and convincing power at the time it was propounded. But its capacity to hold conviction through changing circumstances has proved limited. The virtual dismissal of the Old Testament from the Christian canon is difficult to accept. The whole Bible, New Testament as well as Old, has a strongly temporal sense that is not easy to dismiss. The denial of real significance to the events of contemporary history seems inhuman as well as unbiblical.

None of this refutes Bultmann's theory, and even if his version of the completedness of Christian truth fails, others may succeed. The point here is only that the price of treating the Christ-event as bringing an end to relevant history is high. To argue for renewal as the one and only correct Christian reform at all times and places seems to involve paying such a price. To argue simply that renewal was the appropriate strategy at a particular time and place, such as Wittenberg or Geneva in the sixteenth century, involves no such cost.

If part of the meaning of Jesus Christ is the intensification of hope for a new world, then the history that follows Jesus, viewed from the centrality of Jesus, is a meaningful one. It is one in which the process of transformation continues alongside other processes of unfaithfulness, atrophy, and destruction. In that history transformation continues the work of Jesus and responds to the continuing call of Christ.

I have argued elsewhere (*Christ in a Pluralistic World*) that authentic transformation is what happens when God is effectively present in an event. God's presence introduces a novelty that enables a human being to incorporate elements from the situation into experience in a way that is enriching. However slightly, the person is transformed by that inclusion. God's effective embodiment in the world can be named Christ. Thus Christ is causally present wherever transformation occurs.

We learn this through Jesus, and we have reason to think that the effective embodiment of God in Jesus co-constituted his very selfhood in a way we do not experience in ourselves. In Jesus we encounter the divine transforming power in its fullness, and we are transformed. Part of that transformation is heightened openness to Christ.

The argument that the church needs transforming today does not depend on this Christology. But the plausibility of seeing God at work in the process of transformation can enhance commitment to it. At the same time it should be stressed that renewal also involves the kind of transformation in which God's presence can be discerned. Hence, although this is the final theological argument for the appropriate inclusiveness of this model of church reform, it certainly does not deny the theological value of renewal.

Our Present Goal:
Transformation

That the more inclusive ideal for the church is to transform and be transformed does not settle the question of the appropriate present goal. Perhaps only a church that is secure in its own identity can critically appropriate from others or engage in effective criticism of others. There is strong evidence that the church today does not have that security.

Furthermore, a church now formed uncritically by its cultural environment needs to purify itself before it can critically reappropriate those elements of its culture that embody genuine wisdom or insight. Even if, ultimately, selective learning from others is desirable, it can be argued that, at present, posing it as a goal can only contribute to the loss of Christian integrity. In that case, a period of renewal must precede any further transformation.

It is easy to apply this argument to the current state of the oldline churches. They represent a certain segment of American society at prayer. Most of the beliefs and attitudes of most of the members are shaped more by their location in society, their secular education, the newspapers they read, and the television they watch than by their Christian identity. Most of them can hardly understand what it would mean to reflect on issues *as Christians*. The establishment and strengthening of Christian identity is essential for either renewal or transformation. And whereas transformation seems to assume that identity, renewal aims more directly at its establishment and strengthening.

This case is strong. It may be correct. However, there are reasons for denying that renewal is the best current program.

A major reason for the decline of the oldline churches is the recognition on the part of many of their members that continuation of older patterns would be morally ambiguous or worse. To a considerable extent the patterns in question are very ancient, so that recovering our heritage and deepening our commitments within it does not solve the problem. It might intensify it. Since renewal is not an uncritical return to any particular past form of church life, some form of renewal might avoid the evils. But the accent on renewal is not usually accompanied by a careful explanation of how these dangers are to be avoided.

Renewal, then, does not guard sufficiently against the danger of continuing the evils of which the church has begun to repent. To clarify and concretize this general criticism, we will consider renewal's response to the three examples discussed in chapter 1. The first is Christian anti-Judaism with its horrendous historical consequences.

The major problem with Christian theology in this regard is that it has made universalistic statements about Jesus Christ and salvation that depict Jews as stubbornly rejecting the offer of salvation, thereby condemning themselves to damnation. Their continuing opposition to this universalistic Christian teaching has led them to be seen as enemies of Christ. They were even called Christ-killers.

This problem is neatly finessed by renewal. Renewal stresses that no one is in a position to make universalistic statements. Our Christian concern is to live out of our own world of meanings, not to impose them on anyone else. We expect others to live in their worlds of meaning. None of them can claim truth in the sense of correspondence with an objective reality with which all have to do. Hence Jews cannot be accused of rejecting the One who was to be their savior and the savior of the whole world. Judaism and Christianity are simply different systems of meaning.

Although this certainly deals effectively with much of the problem, it would be too much to say that it is without continuing danger. If within the Christian community we bring up our children on our canonical stories, "the Jews" will continue to appear there as villains. Without any intention on our part, our children's conscious or unconscious image of Jews will be negative.

There is a broader problem. Although sophisticated Christians may understand that the apparently universal meanings in their symbol systems are no longer to be taken universalistically, it will not be easy to communicate this subtlety to all. The statements about Christ that are so central to the traditional system, and that renewal does not intend to revise, clearly suggest that Christ's salvation is available to all, and that no one can be saved in any other way. If the natural implications of the traditional language are to be deflected, this will require considerable time and attention. Socialization into this world of meanings will not do the job, and if carried on without this corrective it will be dangerous.

In general, we should acknowledge that the Christianity in terms of which identity is to be formed by renewal is quite different from traditional Christianity or that of the New Testament. There, the universalistic language had straightforward universalistic meaning. It is the appropriation of ideas from our scholarly culture rather than from this tradition that supports the new program of renewal. There is, therefore, a tension between the use of cultural arguments to justify the program and the denial of any normative role of culture within the program.

Transformation does not appeal to culture at this finally determinative level. It appeals to scripture and tradition. Of course, it knows that the way it reads scripture is informed by a tradition of scholarship that has been influenced by noncanonical sources. It does not seek purity, especially since it does not find purity in the Scriptures either.

But it approaches culture from the perspective of faith rather than determining the proper role of faith on the basis of cultural norms.

Transformation does not abandon universalistic statements. It knows that these are made from highly conditioned perspectives and are always subject to correction. Hence it expresses itself perspectively or confessionally. But when something appears universally true from that perspective, this is put forward as a hypothesis about the way things are, to be corrected by others as they see the need. For example, most Christians hold the hypothesis that Jesus was crucified by the Romans near Jerusalem, and we expect that, viewing the evidence from diverse perspectives, most people will agree. The hypothesis is subject to correction, but it is a theory about the occurrence of an actual event in everybody's real world.

Of course, there are other statements that deal only with matters relevant to a particular community or that are about our own situation and relationships alone. For example, we may confess that we understand the meaning of the Jewish scriptures through the centrality of Jesus and that this leads us to give pride of place to the prophets rather than to the Torah. On such a topic we should never make the universalistic statement that the prophetic writings *should* be given pride of place.

Somewhere between these extremes are statements such as "Jesus is Lord." Clearly Lordship is a relational term, and only for those who follow Jesus is he actually Lord. Yet there are two connotations that are more universalistic, and their abandonment would separate us quite sharply from our heritage. The declaration of the Lordship of Jesus implies that he exercises a certain role or influence whether or not this is acknowledged. It also implies that others are invited to accept the relationship entailed in affirming his Lordship.

To a transformationist it seems better to work with these traditional ideas, including their universalistic implications, than to dismiss these implications in toto. We can then sort out what is universal and what is particular, with the implications for Christian attitudes toward Jews always in mind. It is simply not historically correct to say that the work of Jesus has had effects only on believers. But certainly the effects change when one accepts Jesus' Lordship. Whether the effects of that acceptance would be of benefit to Jews is a separate question. One hypothesis is that through the acceptance of Jesus' Lordship, Gentiles are engrafted into God's covenant with Jews. In that case, Jews have no need of his Lordship.

The issues involved in the second and third examples were treated briefly in chapter 2. The fundamental question with regard to feminism is whether the biblical understanding of women and men is basically adequate in relation to the issues that women have recently been raising. Certainly one can derive from the Bible a much better pattern of relations between the sexes than the one that has in fact dominated the culture or been formulated in the Christian tradition. Women would have much to gain from the adoption of a truly biblical pattern.

But does this Christian patriarchy infused by love suffice? Or must Christians also affirm the claim for full equality not only in the social and economic order, but also in shaping the cultural and intellectual patterns by which we live? If the latter, then we must, for Christian reasons, adopt ideas and ideals that are not fully expressed in the Bible.

It is possible to argue against these feminist demands that they express the individualism and egalitarianism of the Enlightenment, or that they are not sensitive to the nature of healthy community. In such a community there are many roles to be played. All roles should be honored equally, and all persons should be cared for by the community when in need. But it is not possible for all to have just the roles they prefer. Nor can all the roles be up for constant renegotiation. Stable patterns of expectation are required, and one of the bases for diversity of expectation will always be gender. For the sake of the health of the community, all make sacrifices, subordinating their personal preferences to the good of the whole. It is not helpful to concentrate on one's "oppression" and demand liberation. Instead, it is helpful to accept one's role of service to the community and find joy in that even when a measure of sacrifice is required.

Although there is much truth in such a response to feminism, there is a very real danger that it conceals an effort to maintain male privileges at the expense of women. The society reflected in the Bible certainly did so. In the community around Jesus and in some of the early congregations, the radical affirmation of Wisdom or the eschatological climate set aside some of the definitions of role and status, including those governing women. Some of this relative freedom on the part of women carried over into some Gnostic sects, but the church as a whole renewed male domination.

The criticism of feminism would be more convincing if the argument for mutual support through diverse roles were radically separated from biblical patriachalism, if we could make sure that roles of service and drudgery, as well as those of authority, were equally open to members of both sexes. One can justify that equality by using certain scriptures, but one is unlikely to do so if one is motivated only by conformation to the canon. Only when one accepts insights coming out of contemporary feminism is one likely to find that these are supported in scripture. Hence, on the whole, renewal restricts what it can learn from women in ways that seem unjust—and therefore unchristian—to transformation.

Matters are similar with the issue of anthropocentrism and the future of the earth. One can find within the Bible excellent grounds for overcoming anthropocentrism and for care for the earth. But Christians did not do so until the insights of persons outside the church led to accusations against them. The dominant symbol-system of the church had not led those best socialized into it to pay attention to these matters. It is not likely to do so even today.

If those who guide renewal are sensitive to these matters, they can modify the selection of symbols in such a way as to overcome this problem. If renewal engages in this kind of adjustment of symbols in light of concerns raised outside the church, it moves a long way toward transformation. But this is rarely a clear part of the agenda of renewal. If it is not, then the symbol-system into which new generations are socialized will tend to make them part of the problem rather than part of the solution.

A further judgment must be about the seriousness of the problem. Discussion of this question is likely to be viewed by renewal as a cultural matter that is not of concern to the church. But for transformation, there can be no more important discussion. Nothing less than the future of humanity and the other living species is at stake. If human behavior that has been regarded as harmless, and therefore has not been criticized by Christians, turns out to accelerate the destruction of life, then Christians need to engage in new teaching. If in order to do so we must revise some of our traditional symbols, this should be done. For Christians to be preoccupied with questions of our own identity, while the basis for all life on the planet is rapidly eroded, is "Christian" behavior only by a very narrow definition of "Christian."

It can be replied that if Christians become genuinely Christian, we will withdraw from the consumer society. We will act in ways that are in fact highly beneficial to the earth even if our attention is not focused on biological phenomena. There is much truth in that. Whereas it is very difficult to influence public policy, individuals and small groups can, by changing their lifestyles, withdraw their support from the economism whose hegemony threatens the earth. That may indeed be the greatest contribution Christians can make.

Nevertheless, transformationists believe that bringing God's physical creation much more to the center of our theological reflection is important. It provides additional incentive for frugality and also motivation to act in the public world. It can reduce the danger that Christian concern for justice will lead to opposition to those who work for the earth.

Wesleyan Evangelicalism and the Social Gospel Movement: Responses to Lukewarmness

Chapter 1 pointed out that there were periods of lukewarmness in the oldline churches in earlier centuries. It identified two movements that overcame that lukewarmness by convincingly presenting Christian faith as an inclusive way of being in the world that took account of the best thought of its time. In both cases there was a strong sense of that for which it was supremely worthwhile to strive. For John Wesley it was holiness. For the social gospel it was a just and peaceful society in which all could find fulfillment. Wesley's holiness was radically social, focusing on how the individual related to others in love. The social gospel movement called for personal dedication and sacrifice for the cause. Although neither movement emphasized an otherworldly element, neither denied or minimized it. Attention was directed to how we live here and now. A loving God will care for the hereafter.

From our point of view today, there were naive elements in both. Wesley was inadequately aware of the dangers of self-deception and repression of negative feelings. He expected more of himself and others than is truly human. His depiction of complete sanctification could be, and has been, misleading.

The social gospel movement was far too optimistic about unilinear progress toward its goals. Like Wesley, it expected too much from love as human motivation. It underestimated the inescapable roles of power and even violence and the corruption of the virtuous by power. It too much identified the ideals of late nineteenth century United States with universal human goals. It was insensitive to ecological issues.

We cannot make minor adjustments in either Wesleyan evangelicalism or the social gospel and then return to them for revitalization. The situation of our day is too different from theirs. But that does not mean that we cannot or should not aim at the spread of both holiness and justice in a manner that is as integrated as theirs. We must find a way to do so that responds to the challenges of the late twentieth century as effectively as they responded to theirs.

If we succeed, there is a chance of a new revitalization of the old-line churches comparable to that effected by Wesley and the social gospel in their time. That is our goal. Even if we should succeed in this project, we know that in due course the limits of our accomplishment will become apparent. We will not have arrived at final truth! The history of the church will not end with us unless all history ends in disaster. But that is not now our concern. Wesley and the social gospelers did not labor in vain because their days passed. If we can succeed as well as they, we should indeed rejoice.

The primary purpose of this book is to describe our situation and to issue a call for the church to think again. It needs to think its way to an understanding of its message that will communicate conviction and evoke devotion to Christ. For it to command conviction, it must respond not only to questions of credulity posed by science and history, but also to questions of harmful teachings that have been forced on our attention in recent times. This harm has been done both to believers and, through us, to others. This is the formal statement of the need.

The need cannot be satisfied by a professional offering to supply it. Only as Christians recover their identity and their ability to think about the world and themselves in terms of that identity can either renewal or transformation occur. That is the repeated theme of this book.

Nevertheless, there is a danger that the task may appear more difficult than it is—even hopeless. We have for so long retreated from these challenges that we have almost lost the ability to imagine what it would be like to put forth an exciting, demanding claim in the name of Christ. For this reason, I offer an example of where the collective thinking of the church might lead!

Salvation as the Basileia

Perhaps our most serious weakness at present is that we share no clear idea of "salvation." We are vague about the holiness that was salvation for Wesley and the kingdom of God that was salvation for the social gospel movement. We know that the term "salvation" has been identified in existential and in psychological ways, but these seem somewhat limited. We are aware of otherworldly meanings as well, but we are unsure whether we can affirm them confidently. As a result, even if we accept Jesus as Lord and Savior, we do not know what we are saved from or to. The result, again, is lukewarmness.

Let us boldly proclaim an inclusive salvation, the salvation of the world! If we can flesh that out in convincing ways, we can recover the sense of importance that we have so largely lost. We need the collective thought of the church to do so.

In picturing a saved world we can begin with images that come to us directly from the ministry of Jesus. It is a world in which all sins are forgiven; all diseases, healed; all the hungry, fed; all prisoners, freed; all the lonely, visited. Building on these images, our vision of salvation will include much that the social gospel envisaged, corrected and enriched by the work of black and Latin American liberation theologians. It will include the vision of postpatriarchal, nonhierarchical, and nonviolent communities proposed by feminists. It will emphasize the inclusiveness that many of our churches are now seeking to embody.

Our understanding of salvation will be informed by the wisdom of all the great traditions. From Hinduism we learn much about the marvelous possibilities of the human body and psyche. From Buddhism we learn of an enlightenment that leads to wisdom and compassion.

The salvation we envision will include the regeneration of the soil, the purification of air and water, the cessation of global warming, the reforestation of much of the planet, the maintenance of wilderness, and the preservation of biodiversity. It will include an understanding of human wholeness-in-community enriched by a multitude of psychological insights.

Our understanding of salvation will also be deeply inward. It will include an understanding of holiness, interpreted, as by Wesley, as the fullness of love. This will be enriched by the whole history of Christian spirituality as well as what we are learning from other traditions.

It is only as we know ourselves as filled with Holy Spirit that we can experience ourselves as fully participating in God's salvific work.

This is not a complete list of the ingredients in salvation; indeed, a complete list is not possible. But far more important than completeness is the coherence of the vision. We need to see all these elements in their mutually supportive unity. That is a demanding task, one that will itself be carried out in diverse ways. Some of these ways will be in tension with one another. There will be other church members who strongly oppose some elements of this vision, but serious debates are not to be feared or avoided.

The effort to define that toward which all our collective energies can and should be directed is what is important. We can do this in such a way that as we work along many different lines, we are at the same time working together for a common goal. The sense of the church as a context and support for our many, varied tasks can be restored.

It may be objected that this goal is not distinctively Christian, that others can work for it in other contexts. That is not something to deplore. We hope indeed that others will be working for our goal of a world in which God's will is done. We will support them and work with them. Perhaps they will also support and work with us. What is important is not that we have a purpose shared by no one else, but that we genuinely understand our purpose to be Christian. This understanding will occur when we see our hope as a spelling out for our day of what Jesus proclaimed as the "basileia theou."

Basileia is most often translated as "kingdom." This translation, however, has several problems, beginning with its sexist character, which is absent in the Greek. To avoid this *Basileia* is sometimes translated as "reign." But this puts an emphasis on God's controlling power. Better yet is the term "realm," which is gender neutral and not limited to monarchical interpretation. But to speak of the "realm of God" does not make clear that the reference is to this world as we hope it will be.

The most influential and important use of this term attributed to Jesus is in the Lord's Prayer. There the request that the "Father's" Basileia come is parallel to the request that the Father's will be done on earth as it is in heaven. In heaven God's purposes are carried out, presumably, willingly and joyfully by all the heavenly creatures. To whatever extent the Basileia comes, this becomes true on earth as well. It is this for which we pray. Instead of using any of the English translations, we will employ the Greek word to identify the inclusive salvation to which Christians can devote themselves wholeheartedly.

To identify our vision of salvation with what Jesus called the Basileia of God requires that we believe that God is working toward just such an end. For the belief to be convincing to others, and even to ourselves, it must be argued. Many relevant arguments have already been made, but they are often for one part of the inclusive salvation rather than for the whole. Our task is to integrate these into a coherent vision.

In this process we must show in a consistent way how God is at work in all of this. We can do this if we locate the working of God in our own experience and in all events. We can locate it in the moment of calling, directedness, and opening to the other. We can give a coherent account of this element in experience that shows how it transcends the past and is received as grace. We can also show how the transformation thus worked by God moves toward that Basileia described above.

We must also be able to show how the church and its members can work with God toward this Basileia. In very general terms we can speak of a spirituality of openness to God's call and of the empowerment to respond. We can point to many possibilities of service already established in society that in a thousand small ways move in the right direction.

But this is still not enough. In the days of the social gospel, people could see that society as a whole was moving in the direction for which they were working. Hence, there could be a positive connection between their work and the outcome for which they hoped. Two world wars and a depression undercut the enthusiasm for the social gospel partly because they cut this connection. One might still serve one's neighbor in some small capacity, but it no longer seemed to be part of a wider global transformative movement.

Today, even more than then, the world as a whole seems to be moving away from most of the elements in the vision outlined. It is becoming less just and less sustainable. Individually people are more alienated and less secure. Personal holiness seems to become rarer. It often seems that the highest sights we can set realistically are slowing down the rush to oblivion. That is worthwhile, but to work even for that requires some hope for more.

The social gospel was accompanied by a certain measure of serious analysis of what was happening. If we are to be revived by a shared vision of commanding purpose, we must participate in the hard work of determining what structures are blocking movement toward our goal and hastening us in the opposite direction. Clarifying the structural situation and working toward change there do not replace direct service of the neighbor and restoration of bits of land. But unless these local and particular activities are correlated with one another and with theoretical analysis, the oldline churches cannot be taken seriously as a source of hope.

Again, much of the work has already been done. Some of it has been done by Christians, some, by others. If we as Christians know what we seek, we will be in position to appropriate what has been done and to do or commission work as needed.

The uncertainty of the outcome accents the importance of reflection about the persons who participate in the work. What is their "salvation." Is that, also, completely uncertain?

This is a large topic. There is intrinsic satisfaction in working with God in community with others on an overwhelmingly important task. To do this is to live meaningfully. Even defeats and failures, when shared and reflected upon in a supportive context, can be part of such meaningful living. This is enhanced as we feel God's companionship, knowing that God rejoices in our rejoicing and also shares our suffering. It is enhanced further if one understands the presence of God as empowering, as continuing with us even when we sin, as freeing us from guilt, as enabling us to start afresh. There is a vast literature of Christian spirituality that can help the church help its members as they undertake challenging tasks and often face defeat. More basically, the liturgy of the church can, and often does, fulfill this function.

The church can affirm more than this. It can assure us that we belong to God and that whatever happens to us in this life, the belonging continues. We participate everlastingly in the divine life. What we have been matters forever to God. Our efforts are not lost even when they do not attain their hoped-for ends.

Furthermore, this is no time for the church to hold back on its message that this world is part of a larger spiritual reality in which our lives may continue. In academia there is widespread skepticism about "life after death." But outside academia the evidence seems convincing to many. The collapse of the Enlightenment worldview leads in many directions, but among these it can open up a vision in which much that long seemed impossible regains plausibility.

It is not healthy or fruitful to focus on what happens after death when we speak of salvation. But it is also not healthy to avoid serious questions when they arise or to discourage people from discussing personal experiences that fall outside the usual range. The church should become a place where members are free to talk about all aspects of their experience, not least their paranormal and spiritual ones.

This leads to another dimension of personal "salvation"—that of physical and psychological healing. This is returning to the oldline churches after a long exile. It can be part of the recovery of the paranormal and spiritual dimension of life that the oldline churches abandoned during their acculturation by the Enlightenment.

A more important contribution to personal healing than special prayer services may be the revival of vital community within the church. To be part of real community is in itself healing. The church is already host to many such communities, especially those designed to help addicted people. As we become aware that some degree of addiction affects us all, we might move to more serious efforts to include those who are "normal."

A revived church can be both a symbol of the Basileia for which it hopes and a center of activity for that Basileia. These two are not sharply separated. When the church becomes less patriarchal, less hierarchical, more inclusive, and more energizing of its members, it is helping them to gain some of the qualities of life in the Basileia and, at the same time, it is functioning as a symbol of that Basileia. When preaching not only proclaims that Basileia but also helps the hearers to envision it and see how their lives can be ordered to it, the church is both symbol and active agent of transformation.

Testing the Proposal

This set of beliefs and practices would overcome lukewarmness. It might drive some members away. But it might persuade the youth who grow up in the church that continuing participation is of highest importance. And it might attract others. Implementing these beliefs and practices could also evoke from those who remain a level of commitment now generally lacking.

How well would these changes deal with the challenges to which the church has not adequately responded? Does this understanding of salvation require incredible or implausible beliefs? Is it incompatible with the natural sciences or with historical knowledge? Does it violate the historical consciousness? Does it perpetuate anti-Judaism, patriarchalism, or anthropocentricism?

The greatest of these problems is credibility. Sophisticates have long since decided that if God-language is used at all, it refers to human beliefs and images rather than to an actual agent in world affairs. Some academic theologians share this view. If the formulation of a credible theology must remain within parameters of this sort, it can hardly be revitalizing. But for the churches' witness to be credible does not mean that it is believed by all who hear. It means only that it does not require a sacrifice of the intellect to be believed, that it is compatible with such relevant evidence as we have, that it does not violate our finest insights. By such standards the proposal is credible. But the question of God is of such fundamental importance to the church, that chapter 5 will be devoted to it.

What then of anti-Judaism? There should be no problem here. For some Jews, also, hope for a universal messianic kingdom is central. They may work with us in describing what we can envision about that in our time. They may convince us to change some of our images and to make a greater space for their distinctive contribution. We should not object. We hope that our hopes converge.

For some Jews the understanding of God as present and at work in all things will be congenial; for others, not. The Christian doctrine of incarnation has given greater weight to immanence in Christian teaching than it has had in most Jewish thought. But this is a matter only of degree. Many Christians have preferred to continue the emphasis on divine transcendence, and Jews have traditional ways of speaking of God's immanence. In any case there is nothing anti-Jewish about this idea.

Sometimes we Christians identify God-as-incarnate-in-the-world as "Christ." This gives to Christ an objective cosmic role that may seem to make the Jewish rejection of Christ an offense to Christians and hence nourish anti-Jewish feelings. However, if Christians recognize that this is a name that is meaningful to us but not to others, if we recognize that the same features of reality can be identified in other communities in other ways, there should be no such negative result. *We* may in this way see "Christ" as universal savior. But if Jews prefer to call this presence of God in the world Sophia or Shekinah, our difference is only that we recognize and reverence this incarnate presence of God in the world through and because of Jesus. Jews come to it in other ways. Our task is not to agree with Jews or to copy their beliefs and practices. It is to avoid villifying them as we celebrate Jesus as Lord and Savior.

Some Jews might complain that at present the maintenance of Jewish particularity is so important that this Christian universalistic vision is uncongenial. They are free to pursue their goals quite independently. We hope that our pursuit of ours will not impede them. But our heritage is universalistic, and we need not apologize for that because others find it uncongenial in terms of their history, present condition, and needs.

The proposal should not be alienating to Christian feminists. Like some Jews, some feminists want now to concentrate on particularity in separation. But that cannot be the ultimate Christian hope, whether of men or women. And many feminists, even if they see need for some separate work at present, hope ultimately for reconciliation and shared community.

On the whole feminists are presently further along than anyone else in envisioning a transformed world worthy to be called God's Basileia. Hence, a contemporary vision of the Basileia as the salvation we seek is likely to rely heavily on their work. Some may object to our "co-opting" of their insights and imagination, and in that sense this project may be offensive. But once one has published one's work, it is in the public domain and it is unreasonable to object to others being persuaded by it and making use of it.

What has here been named "God" is definitely not stereotypically male. Perhaps it should be named "Goddess" in order to contrast it with the Absolute Ruler that has so often been the image of God. Experiments with language and the liturgy will help. Transformationists believe that we need both to rethink the divine in light of our changing knowledge of the world and also to reimage or reimagine. If we do this, feminine imagery, such as Sophia or Wisdom, will gain a greater role.

Finally, the vision certainly has a place for the contribution of ecology. It may be that the best way to achieve a holistic vision of the Basileia will be to begin with the biosphere, moving from that to its physical and chemical requirements and to discussion of its most important members—human beings. Humanity will not survive apart from the biosphere, and as long as we do not recognize that we are part of this biosphere, the anthropocentrism of our inherited categories of thought is likely to misdirect our energies. All our concerns for justice, participation, and peace and for a nonpatriarchal order can be formulated with respect to the human species viewed as a highly distinct part of the biosphere. This will remind us, in Christian terms, that we are truly creatures and not gods.

4

Realizing Unity
Through Continuing Repentance

In the earlier chapters my concern has been with the restoration of vitality in the oldline churches in a way that is faithful both to Christ and to their own traditions. I have argued for a transformationist approach as adequate to this task. This approach affirms that in the name of Christ we are to be open to learning and to being transformed by wisdom wherever we find it. It also argues that we have responsibility to transform society.

The argument has been addressed to the oldline churches because of their lukewarmness. This lukewarmness has been identified as the deepest reason for their decline. But the oldline churches face another problem that may only be exacerbated by the strengthening of convictions. That problem is division.

Possibilities and Limits of Reconciliation

The division within these churches is sometimes described as one between liberals and conservatives, and those categories are somewhat useful. In view of the survey of the challenges to the oldline churches in chapter 1, however, it will be more useful to describe the churches in terms of their basic responses to these challenges. One group wants to continue the process of repentance, which has gone some distance in all these churches. This group wants to make the reforms that will truly respond to these challenges. The other group sees the substance of the faith already eroded by the responses made to past challenges, and it resists going any further in that direction. The two groups can be called "reformists" and "conservative traditionalists." The word "conservative" is needed because there is a "tradition" of reform as well, and it is not this tradition to which appeal is made.

The most heated debates today are about the ordination of homosexuals. Reformists generally see the oppressiveness of past sexual teachings of the church as one of our greatest crimes. They believe that when we free ourselves from traditional negative attitudes toward sexual activity, love and justice call for ending our long oppression of homosexuals. The church's willingness to give equal place to homosexuals is, for these reformists, a test of its seriousness in proclaiming a gospel of love and justice.

Conservative traditionalists, on the other hand, see our society as having lost its moorings in matters of sexuality. Although they affirm that sexuality is a gift of God and accordingly good, they believe that it should be subordinated to other ends and restricted to traditional channels. They fear that the church has already relaxed its standards too far on this and related issues. To withdraw condemnation of the homosexual lifestyle would be for many the last straw. It would mean that the church had caved in completely to the demands of a decadent culture.

When contradictory positions are felt so strongly, we do not have lukewarmness! The problem for the church is that the intense convictions are not about Jesus Christ, but about a particular current issue. Although supporters of both positions assume that their views are Christian, the virtual absence of theological reflection in the church has led to poor formulations of the Christian reasons for the two positions. Here again we cannot expect much improvement unless the church renews its seriousness about the theological vocation of all believers.

Renewal and transformation are theologically explicit models for revitalization that can only be realized as that vocation is renewed. Either one would provide a fuller Christian context for these debates. However, these contexts would not be neutral. In general, renewal supports limiting reforms and transformation supports continuing them.

The previous chapter gave reasons for supporting the transformation option. One of those reasons is that reforms are needed. Nevertheless, transformation is not simply a justification of all reforms proposed in the name of love and justice. Transformation finds justification for many reforms in the tradition, but it requires that the reforms be theologically justified. Not all proposed reforms are rooted in the tradition, not even the tradition of reforming to which transformation appeals. In some instances transformation sympathizes with the conservative traditionalists in their fear that some proposed reforms simply break with tradition.

Transformation hopes to persuade traditionalists that many reforms are ways of advancing the tradition rather than breaking with it, but transformation holds that this must be shown in each case. Although transformation occasionally sides with traditionalists against reformists, more often it undertakes to offer a third option. An example of that will be given in the last section of this chapter in the discussion of how Christianity is related to other religious ways.

Alongside the transformationist goal of reinvigorating the church in faithfulness to its calling is the goal of reconciliation of opposing groups within it. Transformation recognizes, of course, that it is, in itself, one of the groups within the church making claims that are controversial and potentially divisive. But it hopes that the proposals it offers can in some measure transcend the present divisions and gather a larger consensus. Authentic reconciliation always involves transformation, and transformation hopes that it can assist in reconciling reformists and conservative traditionalists.

The reconciliation that is most needed is between those who have relatively consistent, though polarized, convictions. Of course, the moderate middle should be involved. But the goal is to find a way to do justice to the deepest convictions of both the traditionalists and the reformists, not to find compromises that will avoid institutional splits. Compromise alienates those who have strong convictions on both sides and carries the churches still deeper into lukewarmness.

The possibility of achieving authentic reconciliation lies in the existing unity. This unity is in Christ. Unless both partners to the disagreement affirm Christ as their primary loyalty, there is no starting point for reconciliation as a church. This is an important qualification, because today many in the churches have primary commitments elsewhere. For example, if one of the contestants owes primary loyalty to the advancement of an ethnic group and the other is primarily committed to the maintenance of a Eurocentric society, the fact that both attend church does not provide a basis for reconciliation. We need not exclude such people from Christian fellowship, but they cannot function as the primary representatives of their respective viewpoints for purposes of seeking a Christian position that does justice to both sides.

Even if those whose reconciliation we seek sincerely identify their deepest commitment as Christ, this does not guarantee much agreement. What is meant by "Christ" can vary greatly. For some, "Christ" may function exclusively as a proper name for the Galilean carpenter and what contemporary historical scholarship says about him. For others, "Christ" may identify the second Person of the Trinity and the Word's incarnation, with little reference to the particular character or teaching of Jesus.

Despite the great differences among persons equally devoted to what they understand by "Christ," unity in Christ is not devoid of meaning. Even those with little interest in trinitarian and Christological dogma believe that in some way through Jesus they learn something about God or are related to God's ongoing reality. On the other side, even those whose emphasis is on eternity and the basic structure of the divine drama of salvation recognize that it was in the historical figure of Jesus that this drama reached its climax. The church has affirmed this duality in its Chalcedonian Creed, and whether either side accepts the ancient language of this formulation, both can acknowledge the dual reference to a historical figure and to divine reality.

Such agreement functions only to ensure that the explanation for both traditionalist or reformist views will refer both to what we know of the historical Jesus and to God as known especially through Jesus. This leaves the door open to various emphases: the fact of incarnation, the teaching, the deeds, the personality, the crucifixion, the resurrection, the living Lord, the earliest testimony, or the subsequent creedal formulations. Most Christians can recognize authentic faith in another, even when the locus of emphasis differs.

Furthermore, whether the primary reference is to the historical Jesus or to the divine reality incarnate in him, the whole Bible is brought into play. One cannot abstract what is known of God through Christ from the witness of the Jewish scriptures, nor can one understand the Jewish carpenter apart from his immersion in these scriptures. The appeal to these scriptures adds both to the unity among disagreeing Christians and to the complexity of the arguments through which they explain how their views are faithful to Christ.

The scriptural witness supports both the importance of continuity with tradition and the necessity of repeated reform. Hence, in principle, the rift that threatens us can be overcome. The issue is *what* reform is in faithful continuity with the history of reform that constitutes the tradition at its best. Is the needed reform a cleansing of the church from changes that have infected it? Or is it the introduction of ideas and practices that differ from any found in its past? Careful listening to one another can lead to mutual acceptance as authentic believers, even when acute disagreements remain. Some shared action may follow from the common devotion to Christ despite all the differences.

Furthermore, the possibility exists that mutual understanding and respect can lead to proposals for institutional reform, which are sensitive to continuity with tradition and accepted by both parties as embodying their deepest concerns. It may be possible to change liturgy and church teaching in ways that are truly sensitive to women's experience, for example, without damaging discontinuity with the tradition. It may be possible to think through changes in practice in relation to the natural world that are both continuous with Christian tradition and also substantially reduce the destructive impact of human actions on the environment.

On the other hand, there may be an impasse. The changes the reformists find necessary in faithfulness to Christ may be fundamentally rejected by the conservative traditionalists because of their different understanding of such faithfulness. If each group has come to recognize and respect the Christian authenticity of the other, it may be possible to give space for both groups within a single congregation.

But it may not. It is not possible for one and the same institution both to ordain women and to refuse to ordain women. If some believe that the refusal to ordain women is the only faithful position and others believe that faithfulness requires just that ordination, both groups cannot have their way. Institutional division may be needed to allow each group to express its faith. Better two churches, each of which embodies conviction and expresses that conviction in liturgy and action, than one that is engaged in endless controversy, trying fruitlessly to maintain institutional unity through halfway measures, and thereby fading away into lukewarmness. If the separation is achieved with mutual respect, the deeper unity in Christ is not denied.

A New Christian Ecumenism

Reconciliation or institutional division within the oldline churches is presently the most pressing issue. But transformationists share with many other Christians the goal of a much wider expression of Christian unity. The oldline churches have led in the ecumenical movement of the past century, and we have much to celebrate in our achievements.

At the beginning of the century, most Christians belonged to one of three great branches: the Eastern Orthodox, the Roman Catholic, and the Protestant. Each of these had great suspicion of the others, and suspicion played a large role also in relations among some Protestant denominations.

To an astonishing degree these suspicions have been allayed. There is extensive rapprochement between the Eastern and Western churches. Protestants and Catholics work together on many matters. Among oldline Protestant denominations, mutual respect and cooperation are taken for granted. Councils of churches have become widespread, culminating in the World Council of Churches. In the latter, the younger churches play a role that could hardly have been envisaged at the beginning of the century.

There are, of course, disappointments. Intercommunion, especially between Roman Catholics and others, remains elusive. Despite church unions, the number of Protestant denominations has increased. Further splits may be in the offing over the new issues on which this book is focused. At present the impetus toward further denominational mergers has declined.

But these limitations should not cloud the picture of achievement. Mutual respect and recognition of others as authentically expressing Christian faith have largely superseded exclusivist claims and mutual suspicion. In part, it is success in overcoming exclusivism that has reduced the impetus toward further ecumenical work.

Now that denominations clearly recognize that they are only particular expressions of the one church, they can claim less loyalty. Denominational leaders often find this disturbing. They have become more interested in recovering and reemphasizing the distinctive contributions and emphases of their denominations than in institutional merger. Nevertheless, they take for granted that other denominations, as well as the Roman Catholic and Orthodox Churches, also embody, in particular ways, authentic Christian faith.

During the century in which, for the first time, there has been a great move toward unity of long antagonistic segments of Christianity, major new fissures have developed. While the old animosities based on trinitarian and soteriological issues are healed, new divisions have fractured the unity of Christianity. Ironically, the century ends, as it began, with three great branches of Christianity: one consists in the oldline churches as a whole, which through the ecumenical movement, have become reconciled to one another; another, Pentecostalism; and the third, Fundamentalism. Mutual suspicion among these branches today is analogous to ill feelings that existed at the beginning of the century between what were then the three great branches of Christendom. To the transformationist it appears that this new fracturing of the body of Christ presents a challenge that should redirect the primary energies of the ecumenical movement.

One great division resulted from renewed emphasis on spiritual gifts in the popular life of the church. The charismatic movement within the oldline churches has played a role. But by far the most important developments have been the Pentecostal churches that have become a major factor especially, but by no means exclusively, in Latin America and Africa.

At least at the level of the World Council of Churches, and also by the Vatican, an ecumenical hand has been extended to these churches with modest success. Little more can be expected in the immediate future. Many oldline Protestant denominations, during the period in which they were successful in aggressive evangelistic strategies, showed only secondary interest, at best, in ecumenical relations with other denominations. These issues become more pressing when ecclesiastic communities settled down to a more stable existence. As this happens with the Pentecostal churches, much more ecumenical discussion and cooperation will be possible. This will require an end to class snobbishness and condescension on the part of the older churches, along with a genuine openness to charismatic phenomena that has been missing during their captivity to the Enlightenment. It will require also a willingness on the part of the Pentecostal churches to become self-critical and to engage in new types of theological reflection.

The grounds for hope lie in the origins and history of these churches. The Pentecostal churches grew up around an experience that was not cultivated or even recognized in the established denominations. They are not committed by their experience to opposing the teaching of the oldline churches, except as it excludes that experience. The Pentecostal experience can lead to a measure of spiritual and intellectual liberty as easily as to rigidity and narrow dogmatism.

The origin of Pentecostalism in experience contrasts with that of the other great twentieth-century movement. Fundamentalism arose as a direct attack on the positions and policies of the oldline churches, which were viewed as a betrayal of the faith. The prospect of ecumenical relations with churches that maintain a strictly Fundamentalist posture remains dim. Such churches can sometimes form their own interdenominational alliances, but their self-understanding is incompatible with give-and-take relations with non-Fundamentalist groups.

Nevertheless, there is hope for reducing barriers and attaining mutual affirmation here too. To understand this hope requires a brief review of the context in which Fundamentalism arose and of its subsequent history. In the seventeenth and eighteenth centuries, the church rather easily came to terms with the Cartesian-Newtonian view of the world as a machine. This presupposed a machine-maker who stood outside the machine and occasionally interrupted its normal operations for "His" (the masculine pronoun is appropriate here) purposes. The greatness and complexity of the created order attested to the greatness of the Maker. The one who made the machine could also intervene in its workings; so the supernatural element in Christian tradition could be maintained.

By the nineteenth century, however, this adjustment of Christian teaching to the natural sciences began to break down. The problems were recognized first in German theology, and, in response, Christian teaching was separated from the natural sciences and placed in a different compartment of human knowledge. In the English-language world, objections from the natural sciences were ignored or fended off until the theory of evolution mounted a frontal attack. To this attack, a vigorous response was required.

Given an evolutionary viewpoint, if God's role was the initial creation, then what God created was far less interesting than what evolved from it! Human beings, instead of being created separately in the image of God, were now seen to be just one highly evolved species in the natural world. Evolution took place through the survival of the fittest. Moral lessons were sometimes drawn from this doctrine that were in sharp opposition to Christian teaching of care for the weak and powerless. Finally, there was a direct denial that the story of creation in Genesis provided an accurate account of creation.

One widespread response was to conclude that Christianity as a whole was discredited. Since so much of its previous apologetic was no longer tenable, and since honest openness to science appeared to refute its doctrines, the long decline in Christian credibility accelerated. As a result, in the United States, Christian teaching was by and large ejected from the burgeoning secular universities.

Despite the radical character of the changes required, the oldline churches in general sought to accommodate the factual assertions of the new biology without allowing them to overturn the moral and religious teaching of the Bible. There were two main ways of doing this. One was to follow the German pattern and separate the moral and religious dimensions from the natural dimension, leaving the latter to scientific investigation, and thereby preserving the former for church teaching.

Transformationists, on the other hand, agreed with Fundamentalists in the refusal to segregate theology from knowledge of the natural world. They opposed the Fundamentalist insistence that all necessary knowledge was to be found in the Bible. Hence they developed a synthesis that required transformation both of the scientific worldview and of the Christian tradition. They did this by relocating God's creative action from a single founding event to a continual working in the whole evolutionary and historical process.

In either case, the Bible had to surrender its authority to tell us factually about origins. This surrender was aided by the great accomplishments of nineteenth-century biblical scholarship, which applied secular-historical methods to the ancient texts. With their help it displayed the "evolution" of thought embodied in the Bible itself. Thus there was a close relation between the acceptance of biblical criticism and the acceptance of new scientific theories that conflicted with those that had been drawn from the Bible.

The joint acceptance of critical biblical scholarship and evolutionary theory by leadership in the oldline churches understandably provoked a crisis. This "Modernist" understanding of the Bible and the world was a sharp break from the traditional one. The understanding of basic religious concepts such as salvation was affected by the change. In short, Modernism was a truly revolutionary development in the thought of the oldline churches in the United States.

The response of the majority of those who remained in the church was moderate and mediating. Most people accepted some distinction between scientific and religious teaching without knowing much about the historical criticism of the Bible. They preferred to minimize the difference between an evolutionary account of creation and the biblical one.

Still others saw Modernism, and the halfway houses and compromises of the moderates, as faithless to Christ. They reaffirmed unqualified commitment to all those doctrines that were being questioned, calling these "the fundamentals." Fundamentalists thus uttered a flat no to all the adaptations to historical and scientific knowledge that were made by Modernists and moderates. To block all the loopholes employed by their opponents, they developed doctrines of biblical authority that were more rigid than any previously devised. Because they believed the Genesis account of creation must be literally accurate, they disputed the evidence for evolutionary origins that conflicted with it, arguing that all valid evidence could be read instead in "creationist" terms. They claimed that this was a scientific theory as well as Christian dogma. In this way, they continued the received Christian tradition little changed in content, although considerably rigidified.

Many of those who were convinced that Modernism had abandoned much that was precious to the Christian, and hence followed Fundamentalist leadership, nevertheless found unattractive the preoccupation with refinements on the doctrine of inerrancy and disputes with the dominant community of scientists. They wanted to proclaim positively what they believed to be the Good News of Jesus Christ in a way that was faithful to the spirit as well as to the letter of the Bible.

As a result, there have been encouraging developments within churches with Fundamentalist histories. The most distinctive Fundamentalist doctrine, biblical inerrancy, has provoked extensive discussion. Alternative interpretations of what is inerrant and of what inerrancy means are considered. There are also those who move away from the language of inerrancy altogether. Many have rejected the label "Fundamentalist" in favor of "conservative evangelical." Under this label they have been joined by others who do not have Fundamentalist backgrounds. The spirit and vitality that characterize much of conservative evangelicalism are often the envy of mainstream members of the oldline churches.

Meanwhile Modernism was largely superseded in the oldline church leadership by Neo-Orthodoxy or Neo-Reformation theology. Especially with theologian Karl Barth, this involved a high view of biblical authority. Although Fundamentalism was initially suspicious of Barth because he did not reject biblical criticism in its entirety or affirm biblical inerrancy, eventually Neo-Orthodox views of biblical authority came to have a place in formerly Fundamentalist quarters. For example, in his book *After Fundamentalist,* Bernard Ramm, well respected by Fundamentalists, recommended Karl Barth's view of biblical authority.

There are thus indications that much of what was the Fundamentalist movement may move toward a posture of openness to interaction with oldline churches. Mutual acknowledgment of authentic faith, mutual respect, and considerable cooperation may become possible, as the issues that first set off the Fundamentalist reaction recede to the background. Achieving ecumenical relations among oldline, Pentecostal, and post-Fundamentalist Christians in the next century is the same sort of challenge as achieving such relations among Orthodox, Catholics, and Protestants was for this one. It will require the same kind of theological reflection in the churches that made possible the great ecumenical advance of the twentieth century.

One Way among Many

Christianity today finds itself in a world in which it is but one way of salvation alongside other religious traditions, which claim equal status with us. As we live day by day beside members of these other communities, we recognize the authenticity of their claims. As we study their traditions, we discover profound wisdom that is often quite different from that which we gain from our own canon.

As a result, many members of the oldline churches are beginning to believe that Christianity's relation to the family of religious traditions is similar to the denomination's relation to the family of denominations and churches that make up Christianity as a whole. They look for a common ground, and then elevate it to the central object of commitment. Focusing on Christ, then, seems parochial and is replaced by a focus on what is thought to be a universal divine reality, which is diversely named in the traditions.

This reformist attitude and proposal have many admirable characteristics. They encourage a spirit of mutual affirmation and acceptance. They bring an end to Christian arrogance and imperialism. They prepare Christians to learn from others.

Nevertheless, this attitude is founded on an erroneous judgment. The relation among the great religious communities is not like that among the Christian bodies. In the latter case, all have a common origin and look back to that origin as authoritative. Despite diverse interpretations, there is a common affirmation of the centrality of faith in Jesus Christ. The diverse religious traditions, on the other hand, do not have a common origin or a common object of devotion. Although there may be features shared by all of them, these features do not constitute what is of supreme importance to any of them. These features can establish a measure of kinship and even an opening for mutual understanding, but they cannot assume the role in interfaith relations played by Christ in the Christian ecumenical movement.

Does this mean, then, that Christians must view other traditional ways as false, or even evil, despite appearances to the contrary? Since our ultimate loyalty is to Christ, must we see ourselves in competition with those who have other loyalties? Does our faith establish a negative relationship toward those who do not share it? As we become more deeply Christian in our beliefs, are we thereby further separated from those who do not share them?

We seem to face a dilemma. If we are to establish common ground with followers of other religious ways, we must relativize our faith in Christ. If we remain firm in our devotion to Christ as universal Savior and Lord, we must deny the value and validity of all other traditions.

However, transformation offers another option, one that both emphasizes Christ's radical salvific uniqueness and also opens us to a positive attitude toward other traditions. We ask, first, how salvation is to be understood. The preceding chapter proposed that it is the Basileia, proclaimed and foreshadowed by Jesus, the world in which God's will is done. Here and now we can participate in the continuing work of Christ directed toward that salvation. There is thus a preliminary salvation in this coworking with Christ, and in fragmentary ways the Basileia is already present. Thus we look back to Jesus Christ as our Savior. We experience salvation here and now. We look forward with hope to the full and inclusive salvation envisioned as the fullness of the Basileia.

Given this understanding of salvation, how are we to understand other religious traditions? Since our relation with Israel is of such central importance for us, we will begin with that.

The life of Israel with God was markedly different from that of any other people. This does not mean that God was absent and inactive elsewhere in human history. To assert that would be to deny that Israel understood God rightly. Nevertheless, the salvation we have received and are receiving, and for which we hope, is bound up with Israel's history. Jesus' work cannot be separated from this context. Nevertheless, in order to become Savior of the world, he transcended this context as well.

In and through Jesus this salvific working of God broke radically through ethnic boundaries. In and through the Christ-event, Gentiles in large numbers became engrafted into the history of God's saving work in Israel. Furthermore, although most of the ingredients of Jesus' message and even of the interpretations of Jesus' person and work may be found in Jewish traditions prior to, and independent of, Jesus, the Christ-event as a whole introduced a new understanding of salvation that has marked the Christian community. For example, for us, the cross, for good or ill, plays a role it had not played in Israel before Jesus and has not played there since. Christianity cannot be separated from its literal and symbolic meanings.

Thus Christians are not *only* engrafted into Israel. We are also called and shaped by the Christ-event in new ways. The way God has continued to work salvifically in Israel is not identical with the way God has worked in the church. We hope that some day Israel will reclaim Jesus as its own, that its inclusion of Jesus will play a role in shaping the future Israel's experience of God's salvation. We know that we Gentiles are already benefiting from recent Jewish studies of Jesus that foreshadow such a reclamation by Jews, and we can hope that as Jews continue to reclaim the Jewish Jesus, we Christians will come to a fuller understanding of God's intentions for us as well.

Clearly our relation to Judaism is fundamental, intimate, and unique. How we understand this relation has been, from the first, central to the theological tradition. Our errors in defining it have cost us dearly. They have been disastrous for Jews living in our midst.

If we understand salvation in this way, then, are there other "saviors" in human history? I do not think so. We can detect Christ's saving work everywhere, but many follow spiritual leaders whose purposes and goals are not identical with what we understand by salvation. They have not located themselves in a biblical type of salvation history.

There is another and quite different question. Can persons outside the Jewish and Christian communities contribute to salvation? Here the biblical example of Cyrus is pertinent. Certainly he contributed to the salvation of the Jews from exile. For this he could even be called a "savior."

In our context of world religions, the question is whether key figures in other religious communities *contribute* to what we Christians know as salvation. To that question the answer is resoundingly, yes. There is much in other traditions that contributes to realization of a world in which God's will is universally done.

Many of the contributions of other religious ways parallel what we already have in Israel and in Christianity. Something like the Golden Rule can be found in many traditions. Hans Küng has recently formulated an extensive global ethic to which representatives of many traditions have found it possible to subscribe. He believes, with justification, that peace among the religions is essential to world peace. He also believes that such peace can be advanced as we recognize how far we can go together in supporting movements toward justice, righteousness, sustainability, and human dignity. If we assume that peace, rather than conquest, is the way to the Basileia, then all the teachers in other traditions who have sown the seeds of peace have contributed to salvation.

Is the only contribution that other traditions make to the coming Basileia one that we can also make? No! In the case of Israel, Paul specifically told us to expect something more of the Jews, and we have already begun to benefit from their fresh contributions to our understanding of Jesus. We know they have much other wisdom that will contribute to the Basileia.

Paul knew nothing of Islam, and next to nothing of the religious traditions of India and China. But when Christians later discovered them, they learned from them much that they had not previously known. As time has passed, some Christians have abandoned their faith in order to benefit more fully from the wisdom of other great traditions. Other Christians have appropriated from them elements that could be incorporated into their own tradition.

One of the most interesting illustrations of this dual process is found in the relation of Christianity and Buddhism. Especially in its Zen form this has been presented persuasively by such great missionaries to Christendom as D. T. Suzuki. Millions of non-Asian Americans have been deeply influenced. Some have converted from Christianity to Buddhism. Others, such as Thomas Merton, have believed they could be Buddhist as well as Christian. Some of these have introduced Buddhist practices of meditation extensively into Catholic monasteries.

Another form of Buddhism is to be found in South Asia. There, Buddhist leaders have a stronger sense of responsibility for their whole societies than has been common in China and Japan, where this role has been played by Confucianism. For example, Sri Ariyaratne has led what is surely one of the most impressive programs of social action anywhere in the world. His followers spend their mornings in meditation in order to free themselves from the ego that can otherwise so easily taint and distort their action. What they are doing in Sri Lanka is on the way to the Basileia. It also is instructive for others. How much more effective would much of our Christian activism be if it were less distorted by ego-involvement!

At quite another level, Christians are learning much from Buddhism that aids us in our own working for the Basileia. For historical reasons, Christianity formulated its theology chiefly in Greek categories. Much of this was beneficial, for the Greek language was richly nuanced. But the union of biblical and Greek thinking entrenched a destructive dualism between spirit and flesh, soul and body, humanity and nature, subject and object. Today, many Christians want to free themselves from these dualisms, but dualism is so pervasive in Western thought that it keeps reappearing in theology as well.

The most thorough effort in human history to purge thought of dualisms of this sort was that of Buddhists. Two-and-a-half millenia ago, they saw how pervasively dualistic language and thought shaped human life and civilizations. Hence, they did not treat it as a particular problem for Indians or Chinese, but rather as a human one. Their analysis of the problem of dualism and of the destructive effects of dualistic thinking, as well as the spiritual practices through which they freed themselves from this thinking, are unique in their profundity and effectiveness.

My argument, then, is that there is much in Buddhism that contributes to the salvation of the whole world identified as the Basileia proclaimed by Jesus, much that is absent from the Jewish and Christian traditions. For Christians to refuse to profit from this wisdom because it comes to them from outside their own tradition would not be an expression of faith. Instead it would express defensiveness. If we trust Christ and seek to be coworkers for the Basileia, we will gratefully accept whatever can help us in our task. We can affirm Gautama as the unique teacher and embodiment of Enlightenment, in other words, as the Buddha.

In a similar way we can affirm Moses as the Lawgiver and Muhammad as the Prophet. To call Jesus Savior of the world in no way denies that Gautama is the Buddha; Moses, the Lawgiver; or Muhammad, the Prophet. Furthermore, if the salvation Christ proclaimed and foreshadowed is to be realized, those who witness to it and seek to cooperate in its service should be open to all that God has done in the world in other communities as well as ours. Without the contributions of others, the full actualization of the Basileia will remain an idle dream.

That God has worked and is working among people outside the church as well as among those within it should be no surprise to a reader of the Bible. That what God has accomplished in other communities supplements and enriches what we have inherited through our own tradition in no way diminishes the unique importance and saving value of that tradition. It does warn against an idolatrous attitude toward it. The great strength of our tradition is that it points us forward to a future that transcends past and present, one that can be enriched by the contributions of all people.

Universalistic Claims

This understanding of the relation of Christianity to other religious ways involves universalistic affirmations about Jesus Christ as Savior. Just such universalistic claims have been at the heart of Christian anti-Judaism. We have from the beginning of this book taken the overcoming of Christian anti-Judaism as an imperative requirement for the oldline churches, a test for all their theology. Renewal deals with this problem by abandoning universalistic claims in general. Transformation questions the efficacy of that strategy and sees the price of such abandonment as too high. It proposes to distinguish carefully between universalistic statements and those that have their meaning only within limited contexts. It then proposes to transform the universalistic affirmations so that both their perspectival character and their openness to correction will be clear, and they will be free from the damaging consequences of past formulations.

The perspectival character of the claim that Jesus is the Savior of the world is evident. This is a statement that will be made only by those with a certain understanding of salvation, namely, one shaped by Israel's history read through the Christ-event. This evident perspectival character may suggest that the meaning of the statement is exhausted in its relations to other features of the Christian symbolic system as renewalists assert. In that case it has no universalistic implications.

But to a transformationist that seems erroneous. What Christians mean by salvation can be explained to others. It can be understood by them. Given that meaning, the claim that Jesus is uniquely related to that salvation can also be understood. Others can discuss and criticize that claim, and Christians can benefit from what they say. We can revise our formulations based on what we learn in these discussions. To affirm the perspectival character of one's assertions is not to abandon universal intentions, but it is to hold one's judgments subject to correction by what is seen from other perspectives.

It was noted above that the universalistic claim that Jesus is Savior of the world does not conflict with the universalistic claim that Gautama is the Enlightened One—the Buddha. Indeed, it leads to acceptance of that claim. When the universalistic meaning of the claim that Jesus is Savior of the world is carefully explained, Buddhists could, in principle, accept it. However, because of the common absolutist connotations of "salvation," they may prefer to state what they accept in different terminology.

The connotation they would not accept is that of supreme importance. Even if it is the case that there is a unique relation between Jesus and the Basileia that the Christian identifies with salvation, the Buddhist may hold that orienting one's life toward the future in that way is unwise, that it interferes with the attainment of Enlightenment. Thus, agreement about universalistic claims does not entail agreement about their implications for human life.

At this point it is best for Christians to recognize a deep pluralism and to draw back from pressing our universalizing proclivities. Our tendency is to state that all people *should* orient their lives to the realization of the Basileia. But that may well be a continuation of Christian arrogance and imperialism. Perhaps we should only confess that through Christ *we* are drawn to orient our lives in that way. We listen, then, to others who are drawn to the attainment of Enlightenment. Since we can see their attainment of Enlightenment as in fact a contribution to the realization of the Basileia, we can recognize this difference without negatively judging the alternative goal and life orientation.

What about the danger of anti-Judaism? If Jesus is the Savior of the world, and if what we mean by salvation is informed by the Jewish tradition, then are we not judging that those Jews who rejected Jesus and maintained their separateness as Jews made a fundamental error? If so, are we not again authorizing a polemic against them? Given the past consequences of the universalistic claim for Jesus as Savior, would it not be better to avoid it altogether?

Unless the transformation of the meanings of "salvation" and "Savior" that have been proposed become truly effective, the argument against the use of these terms by Christians is strong. Christians could assert less dangerously that there is a unique relation between Jesus and the Basileia he proclaimed, and that we find meaning and value in involving ourselves in that relation. Jews would have no reason to object to Christians thinking and acting in that way and little to fear from its consequences.

Transformationists, however, are not satisfied. We recognize with renewalists the power and importance of the language of the tradition. To abandon it is to leave its meanings unchanged. The fact that a few Christians ceased to use some central terms would do little to affect Christian attitudes toward Jews. Even if this were our only concern, and it is not, the transformation of inherited meanings is more promising than abandonment of the language.

We can go on to point out the important role played by a separate Jewish community in the movement toward the Basileia. We can describe the continuing salvific efficacy of their covenant with God. We can affirm the ongoing contribution of their independent reflections about the messianic age to our developing envisagement of the Basileia. We can see, therefore, that a division among the Jews, with some initiating the Christian movement—with its far greater inclusiveness of Gentiles—and others continuing in independence and separation, is a double contribution to the salvation we seek. We may regret the polemics between these two groups of Jews in the years following Jesus' death and resurrection and painfully acknowledge the increasing viciousness of this polemic by Gentile Christians in later centuries. Our transformed reading of this history and interpretation of our basic symbols will embody our repentance.

There are no perfect solutions to our problems, but we do not need perfection. We do need a way of enthusiastically and wholeheartedly affirming our faith that does not continue to vilify Jews, oppress women, and discount the natural world. This affirmation of faith, as this book has argued, can be attained, through a transformationist approach.

At every point this approach requires theological reflection. It does not require massive participation by pastors and lay people in the current discussion among professional theologians, but it does require that we renew the habit of thinking about the issues that confront us self-consciously as Christians. May the time come soon when this habit is recovered.

In a serious sense, this book is a sermon on the text: "Be transformed by the renewing of your minds" (Romans 12:2). Without that transformation the oldline churches will make little contribution to the Basileia proclaimed by Jesus. With it, there will be hope.

5

Addressing People with a Renewed Vision of God

Previous chapters have noted repeatedly that the deepest problem of the church in responding to its current malaise is its abandonment of its theological vocation. Theology has become a university discipline. It produces little literature helpful to those in the pew, and they have ceased to expect help from the professionals. These deal with the problems generated by their disciplines and respond to the intellectual ethos of the universities. Although the professionals have in fact produced some material that could help the church respond to its current challenges, there is no place where the church can receive and consider the proposals.

The answer, of course, must be the rebuilding of structures within the church that encourage thinking about the Christian faith and about the needs of the church and the world from that perspective. That little of this is going on suggests both unawareness of the need and fear of what will happen when basic questions are openly considered. Most of this book is intended to heighten awareness of the need, but it is also important to acknowledge the reality of the fear and a considerable measure of justification for it.

This is not a time when we can expect that people studying a theological problem will come easily to consensus. If they look to university theology for help, they will find chaos. If lay people open up honestly to one another, they will also discover that in this long period of silence concerning the real meaning of our faith, believers have moved in many directions to fill the void. If they consult their pastors, the same diversity will appear.

Formulating a Belief about God

Nowhere is the confusion greater than with regard to beliefs about God. To avoid this confusion some are inclined to formulate Christian beliefs in a way that leaves God out. That is not, however, a basis for consensus, since for many others, indeed for most Christians, our faith is in God, and our worship is directed to God. Just as faith is primarily trust in God; so theology consists first and foremost in beliefs about God. To formulate our Christian beliefs without dealing directly with the question of God is not an option.

Chapter 3 proposed a way of understanding Christian salvation that could inspire confidence and conviction. It dealt only superficially with the question of whether the language about God used in the account of salvation could be credible today. Yet this question is of utmost importance if the church is to evoke serious conviction from its members. If theology is first and foremost about God, then even when it discusses a myriad of other topics, what it says about them is shaped by its explicit or implicit doctrine of God. For example, this book has spoken of the centrality and decisiveness for Christians of faith in Christ. But faith in Christ would be idolatrous if "Christ" is separated in Christian understanding and intention from God. For Christians to put faith in Christ is to put faith in God as embodied and manifest in Jesus. It cannot mean to place faith in an individual human being in separation from God.

When there is vital belief in God, as God is known to us in Jesus or the Christ event, there is likely to be strong conviction about the meaning of life and the mission of the church. When people are confused and uncertain about God, lukewarmness is the likely result. The effort to evade controversy by staying silent about what we really mean by "God" has led to vagueness and uncertainty. There can be no revival of the oldline churches without painful struggle with theology. The question of credibility must be faced.

If the credibility of what is said about God in chapter 3 is judged by its conformation to dominant beliefs among western intelligentsia, the answer must be negative. Few professors in the university are prepared to relate God to their scholarship in any explicit way. They write and teach as if there is no God or, at least, as if God made no difference to the ongoing course of events. The idea that there is divine agency in the world is widely regarded as out-of-date.

If the church speaks of God at all, and wishes not to offend the dominant mind of the university, it must allow the word *God* to function as a symbol open to an endless variety of interpretations, many of which will exclude any reference beyond human language. This seems to be the strategy actually adopted by many oldline churches. The church then remains credible by leaving its language open to whatever interpretation the hearer wishes to place on it.

Credibility is thus bought at the price of any possibility of unifying conviction. Although individuals and groups within the church may have convictions and still be able to share in the life of the church, the sharing is not on the basis of their convictions. This sharing does nothing to prevent the church from becoming lukewarm.

Another solution is to reassert the teachings, or at least the language, of the tradition. Even many who do not find traditional beliefs convincing are likely to tolerate this. Many of us say things in the recitation of creeds and traditional prayers, as well as in the singing of hymns, that we do not really believe, or whose serious acceptance would require considerable interpretation on our part. This is a way of maintaining a measure of peace even though it does not inspire conviction.

If we are to elicit conviction, despite all difficulties and dangers, we must find a new consensus. We must find a way of speaking of God that is not incredible, at least in the sense that it does not seem nonsensical on its face, or contradictory of scientific knowledge or human experience. But we must not require that it be acceptable to the majority of intellectuals. That would be an impossible demand in the current intellectual climate. Credible means subject to belief by an open-minded person. It does not mean convincing to all. Affirming God at all in our time is an act of courage and risk. It is an act to which the church should be committed.

In any case, transformationists aim not only at transforming the tradition through what can be learned from external sources, but also at transforming the wisdom of the world. The current state of the intelligentsia is not a happy one. The course of western intellectual life has led predominantly to dead ends. The church as heir to a great tradition has its own wisdom to offer.

Its contribution cannot consist in replacing the results of scientific investigation with biblical ideas. That would be terribly damaging, if it were possible at all. In any case, it would not be transformation, any more than replacing the church's tradition with something different is transformation of that tradition. Transforming the still dominant Enlightenment worldview is possible only as that worldview is deeply understood and then modified. Such modification is now occurring through scientific advances, as well as through other cultural developments. The emerging "postmodern" vision can be enriched and transformed by elements of the church's wisdom that are relevant to it, but not otherwise included in it. This includes above all the understanding of God revealed in the Christ event.

To integrate the Christian faith with the best of current thinking leaves neither unchanged. If the work is done well, it may attract some who are weary of the nihilistic tendencies of the contemporary intellectual world. It may attract others who find that most of the new spirituality associated with the postmodern understanding of the world is superficial. At any rate it should inspire new confidence and conviction among Christians. Instead of feeling defensive about our faith, we can believe that we are part of shaping the emerging vision of reality and a healthy response to that vision.

Despite the intellectual problems and the uncongeniality of any serious affirmation of God in the university, there are cultural currents that both encourage this undertaking and make it urgent. Most Americans assert their belief in God, however varied their beliefs may be. The issue then, sociologically speaking, is more one of contesting for a truly Christian understanding of God than of simply affirming God in general.

Belief in God is a powerful force for evil as well as good. It functions as often to make nations and conventional values sacred as to challenge them and make them relative. It turns attention away from the earth to another, more spiritual, realm, as often as it directs concern to what is happening to God's creatures here and now. Sometimes it is used to claim authority for a charismatic leader beyond any justification. It can support a harsh morality insensitive to the needs of real people. It can become a club with which to attack one's opponents or to condemn those whose views are not socially approved. It can lead to resignation to evil as easily as it leads to a struggle against it. It can lead to false expectations followed by a destructive disillusionment. It can cause a psychologically unhealthy dependency that blocks maturation. The opposition to belief in God among intellectuals stems as often from accurate observation of the harm that such a belief can do, as from adoption of worldviews that do not allow God a place in reality.

When groups within churches seriously discuss their beliefs about God, their primary focus should be on explaining how these beliefs are Christian and revising and reforming them by this criterion. Credibility should be the secondary issue. But since any genuinely Christian belief must be open to checking by whatever evidence there is, credibility, too, must play a pervasive role.

Some Christians are still shaped in their thinking about God by the deistic model of the Enlightenment. God in this model is the Creator of a world machine on which "He" imposes the natural laws discovered by science. The primary relation of this God to human beings is also as Lawgiver, although in this case the laws are moral ones, which we have the freedom to obey or disobey. Judgment in the form of rewards and punishments belongs to the afterlife.

For a long time, with many variations in detail, this provided a consensus for popular thinking about God in this country, which is still prevalent today. Indeed, some scientists reflecting about the implications of the Big Bang theory have given it new life.

Although, in our oldline churches, most people have left this kind of thinking behind, the church has given them little help in replacing it. The question is whether now, belatedly, the process of reconceiving God in a way that can be meaningfully grasped by thoughtful people can begin. Can another consensus be formed? We do not know the answer to this question, because we have not tried to find such a consensus. We have left the shaping and reshaping of belief in God to conservatives on the one side and to the popular media on the other.

The time may be ripe for the oldline churches to accept the leadership role in this rethinking. There is more and more awareness of the need. A new post-Enlightenment worldview is emerging that seems more open to distinctive aspects of the biblical vision. A strong and clear message from the church would have a greater chance of being heard than has been true for decades.

Reclaiming the Mystery,
Spirit, and Wisdom of God

What then can we say? First, we can agree with the older tradition about the mystery of things. The emerging worldview is far more paradoxical, in the sense of not conforming to our expectations, than was the Cartesian-Newtonian worldview it replaces. The world is composed of things that have greater spontaneity and apparent self-determination than the material atoms of the eighteenth century. These things relate to one another with far greater intimacy, and they are less dependent on contact with one another. In short, instead of a world of passive matter on which God imposed laws of motion, we have a world of agents interacting with one another in immeasurably complex ways. Physicists now speak of complexity theory, fuzzy logic, self-organizing systems, and holographic models. No one quite knows what all this means. Certainly no one is able to put it all together into a single, fully comprehensible pattern. But the impression it makes on those who are acquainted with it, even casually, is very different from that of the science of the Enlightenment period.

If God is identified with the deistic God of the Enlightenment, no doubt "He" is dead. To try to fit the Creator-Lawgiver-Judge of the Enlightenment into this new worldview inspires immediate disbelief. It is true that accounts of the Big Bang now suggest that laws, or constants, were established at the outset that are, on the one hand, contingent, and, on the other hand, necessary for the emergence of high-grade organisms such as ourselves. "Contingent" here means not determined by the nature of the entities then existing or by any pre-existing circumstance. It can be interpreted either as chance or as an intelligent decision. The latter choice is highly plausible on the face of it, and the lack of attention to this hypothesis on the part of university theologians results chiefly from the deeply entrenched separation of theology from the natural sciences. For those, and this includes most lay people, who relate what they believe about nature to what they think about theological questions, this lack of support by scholars is no reason to oppose the idea. So there is plausible justification for affirming a role of God in the original determination of the shape taken by our cosmos.

Whatever the future of this speculation, there is space for other hypotheses dealing with the ongoing process initiated by the Big Bang.

In an indeterminate world, there is little place for an all-controlling Will, but there is a place for a persuasive force that provides a measure of order and explains the novelty and self-determination of the world. There is no proof here. Perhaps it is by chance that self-organization generates both order and novelty. Perhaps a measure of self-determination is simply to be attributed to the nature of things with no need to posit any principle, force, or agency as explanation. But there is no inconsistency or contradiction in seeing God present and at work throughout these mysterious processes. Whereas in the Enlightenment worldview God was the external determiner of all things, in this post-Enlightenment world, God is better seen as an active participant in an open-ended creative process.

In such a mysterious world, if we think of God at all, we will certainly understand God to be mysterious. We have no longer any clear knowledge of what the entities making up nature are like. We know that whatever God is, God is not just another such entity located in space-time. Hence, the difficulty of saying what God is like is doubly compounded. But this does not imply blank ignorance or the emptiness or futility of all language about God.

In the Enlightenment era, when Christians searched the Scriptures, they found images of Creator, Lawgiver, and Judge. These were there to be found, and even though they do not leap out at us when we approach the canon today, in the end we, too, must deal with them. What is more likely to commend itself to us today is the image of God as Spirit. The denotation of that word is vague. It suggests mystery, but it is not vacuous. Spirit connotes a presence that is not localized and a power that does not operate by physical force. Although in German our English "mind" and "spirit" are translated by a single word *Geist,* for us "spirit" has the richer connotations. Its meaning does not focus attention on either thinking or feeling, but includes both and more besides. We can apply the term to ourselves, suggesting the elements of aspiration and inspiration and self-transcendence that characterize our human lives. Spirit in us is embodied, although it also transcends our bodies. If Spirit also pervades the cosmos, it may be said to be embodied everywhere, but it also transcends the cosmos.

As human beings, our greatest interest is in how this divine Spirit relates to us. But first we note that whereas in the Enlightenment period the dualism between the human and the natural prevailed, so that this was a completely separate question, in our post-Enlightenment thinking, this dualism is gone. A persuasive account will see God's working in us and in our history as continuous with God's working in cosmic evolution and in every quantum of energy. It will find God in the cells of our bodies as well as in our minds and spirits.

Another scriptural term that we are now recovering is Wisdom. There is a Wisdom at work in the cosmos that vastly transcends any human understanding. This Wisdom is at work in our bodies as well. We may, of course, view our bodies as simply carrying out the "program" that is "imprinted" in the genes. But this deterministic thinking seems to be as much a carryover of the Enlightenment worldview with which science was so long associated as based on the evidence before us. There seems, on the contrary, to be a measure of creativity in our cells as well as a Wisdom that works in and through them to accomplish the miracle of the human body. If we attend to that wisdom, we can trust it and learn from it. Our bodies embody a Wisdom not available to us otherwise. They are not objects to be manipulated and controlled but partners in our life with God.

Many scholars think that the ode to the Word in John 1 was originally addressed to Wisdom. It is, at any rate, remarkably suggestive of how we may think of God's presence in the world today. It begins by affirming that Word or Wisdom played a role in all creation whatsoever. It goes on to suggest a special role of Wisdom in living things. Indeed, it is the life of all that lives. Finally, it expresses itself in human understanding. In short, the same divine reality that enlivens the world enlightens the human soul. There is continuity, but there is also a deepening presence.

The climax comes, of course, in the assertion that this same Wisdom was embodied in a particular man, Jesus. That means that it is in and through him that we gain a clearer view of what this Wisdom is and how it operates in human life. This revelation was not thought of originally, and should certainly not be thought of today, as a body of information that is to be accepted on authority. Quite the contrary, to affirm it is to confess that in encountering Jesus, features of reality that have been unnoticed become apparent, that we become aware of possibilities we have neglected, that we have new awareness of the divine.

Over the centuries the church has taught that Jesus reveals God, but it has in fact constructed most of its teaching about God from other sources. This was true, certainly, of the Enlightenment theology. Reading the story of Jesus does not place God's role as initiating the existence of the cosmos. Nor does God appear strikingly as Law-giver and Judge. These ideas are not denied, but what comes to the fore are compassion and self-giving, even suffering for others. There is calling, and disappointment when there is no response. God is depicted and represented as caring for all things in a profoundly intimate way, and especially for human beings. We are shown a God in whom we can trust completely, but we are not shown that trust and obedience will save us from suffering and untimely death. There is no close connection, in Jesus' vision, between what one deserves and what one receives in these terms. Jesus did not attribute sickness or accidents to sin, and he taught that God sends the rain on just and unjust alike.

Although Jesus saw no necessary justice in the present course of worldly events, he believed that God willed a quite different situation in which all this would be reversed. He both taught and, in his actions, revealed that God is on the side of justice and that God calls us to be on that side as well. Jesus was no "respecter of persons," and he was sure that this was true of God as well. We are called to concern ourselves especially with the downtrodden and oppressed, whom the great of this world ignore or despise.

It is difficult indeed to see a movement toward justice in the working of the Spirit, Wisdom, Life, or Love in the cosmos. God's concern for that can only be discerned in the calling that we experience. Jesus instructs us to pray for the Basileia. As we give ourselves to that call, we can know divine encouragement and empowerment.

We see great power in God as revealed by Jesus. But this is not what most people, even today, think of as power. The common image of the exercise of "power" is control. That on which the power is exercised acts according to the will of the one who has the power. Some such power is exercised by Jesus over the demons. But in his relations with people, Jesus uses his power in other ways. He uses his healing power to work with the faith of others in accomplishing their hopes. His power as teacher lay in his ability to widen people's understanding, to break through restrictive habits of thinking and seeing, and to evoke response. In short, the power of Jesus' teaching lay in expanding the freedom of the hearer and in persuasion with respect to how that freedom might be used.

Jesus called and invited. He did not compel. For him the use of coercive power was a temptation. His power was the power of truth and example. Its supreme expression was on the cross. As Paul understood so well, Jesus' power was what the world calls weakness. But as John saw, through Jesus' crucifixion he exercised an attractive power on the world.

It would be foolish to read a statement about God's power directly off the record of the human Jesus. But it has also been a mistake for the church to ignore its own teaching about revelation so extensively. Omnipotence in any ordinary sense is not what Jesus reveals about God's power. One expects instead to find God calling us, directing us, empowering us, expanding our understanding and our freedom. We would expect to find God seeking our good and working with us in its achievement. We would expect to find ourselves understood, and loved, and supported. We would expect to experience God more as companion than as judge.

On the other hand, it would be a mistake to think of Jesus as "nice." He could be harsh in his denunciations. Although the force he used to drive the money changers out of the temple must have been primarily moral, he is depicted as employing a whip. There is no reason from the revelation in Jesus to suppose that the cosmic working of Spirit or Wisdom is "nice." Indeed, it is not. Life feeds on life. Some are called to play roles that involve suffering and death. There is no assurance that our sacrifice will be appreciated or even noticed by other people. God will know.

If we think in this way, some will follow Jesus in addressing God as Abba. That is a masculine term, but it connotes attributes of the male—tenderness, presence, and care—quite different from those classically associated with God. Those same attributes, however, can easily evoke feminine imagery. If God came to be thought of widely in the ways proposed, gendered imagery in general might decline, and its use would be likely to become more balanced between the two sexes. Obviously the Spirit that pervades the universe is not gendered or more like one sex than the other. And if Wisdom is gendered, it will be feminine.

It was noted that the Enlightenment characteristics of God—Creator, Lawgiver, and Judge—do not stand out when we study the revelation in Jesus in light of the changing view of reality. Nevertheless, for Jesus too, no doubt, God was Creator, Lawgiver, and Judge. Can we make sense of this language also?

Reflection on the Big Bang has restored for some the meaningfulness of the literal idea of God as Creator out of nothing. Certainly this cannot be excluded. On the other hand, the biblical vision of God as Creator emphasizes more the process of ordering and inspiriting the chaos. It does no injustice to the biblical record, or to what we can conjecture from Jesus' thought, to emphasize more God's continual creative work than the once-for-all completed act of creation associated with the Enlightenment worldview.

That God established certain constants that are embodied in all creaturely activity is an idea consonant with what is scientifically known. In this sense God is Lawgiver. But the idea of physical laws is not a biblical one. Biblically, the giving of law has to do with the Torah, the Jewish law. Jesus would never have questioned that God gave this law, but what is striking is the impression that he minimized the value of rigid obedience to it. The life for which he called is not characterized by detailed obedience, but by trust and love. The "law of love" sums up all that is needed. The actual consequence was that Christians have set much of the Jewish law aside and have in general sought salvation in another way. The image of God as Lawgiver need not be rejected, but it must be interpreted in terms of other, more basic, images.

There is finally the question of God as Judge. Jesus certainly understood God as Judge. However, we are not to emulate God in this respect but to leave judgment to God. The reversals that occur in the Basileia are part of God's judgment. They are based on how people deal with one another, especially with the needy.

The Synoptic Gospels also portray Jesus as speaking of judgment at death. Again, in the parable of Lazarus and Dives, what is most striking is the reversal of fortunes and that punishment is for failure to meet the needs of the poor. How literally Jesus took the ideas of Abraham's bosom and fiery torment is difficult to guess. How he related these notions to the coming of the Basileia is equally puzzling. Perhaps the images tell us more about the imagination of a later generation than about Jesus himself. In any case we can learn the lesson of the parable without ourselves adopting the details of the picture or the notion of eternal torment that seems implied.

A clue to understanding judgment may be found in another story, that of the rich young ruler. Here the relation between riches and judgment is made clear with a man who is virtuous by all normal standards. He longs for a fulfillment his riches and his virtue have not made possible. But when Jesus tells him that to find that fulfillment he must free himself of all his wealth, giving it to those in need, he cannot. He goes away sorrowful. His bondage to his possessions prevents the attainment of happiness.

Jesus does not punish him or suggest that he will be punished hereafter. Indeed, there is no imposed punishment at all. The ruler's judgment is inherent in his inability to respond to Jesus' invitation to follow him, and he knows it. Here we see the reversal of fortunes that occurs already here in the midst of present life. Perhaps we can project that into the Basileia or into life after death. There the profound emptiness and misery of a life dependent on controlling power and possessions must stand in stark contrast to the joy of one dominated by love. This kind of judgment is fully compatible with a God whom we are taught to know as Love.

Defining Salvation

This is not intended as a comprehensive doctrine of God. It leaves many questions unanswered. An unfinished teaching, inviting all believers to share in its formulation, may be the best the church can offer today. Perhaps, indeed, it cannot offer that much. Perhaps what has been said above will not commend itself to other believers in our time. It is proposed to elicit response and to encourage others to try their hand.

Some, no doubt, will find that it says too much, goes too far beyond what we can know with confidence. It assigns God a central role in the cosmic process from which many have assumed that God has been evicted. It proposes real efficacy of God in the ordinary functioning of the human body and mind, whereas many suppose we can only discuss the effects of belief in God.

Others will certainly think it says too little. It says nothing about God's absoluteness, immutability, omnipotence, and so forth. It does not guarantee the coming of the Basileia independent of our involvement. It does not guarantee the imposition of punishments on sinners.

All these matters are important and deserve discussion. If the church will reclaim its theological vocation, this discussion will ensue. The proposal here is that we seek consensus first around ideas that fit the post-Enlightenment worldview and the revelation in Jesus. That will already involve major, unprovable, even if credible, claims.

They will need to be tested in the life experience of believers. Out of such testing and discussion can come revisions and expansions.

There is no possibility that all the members of the oldline churches can share in this or any other consensus. Commitments to diverse views are too strong, but total agreement is not required. It would even be dangerous. The teaching of the church needs searching criticism, which comes best from those who disagree. The social gospel, to use again the example of a movement that successfully revitalized the oldline churches, always had critics, including strong opponents, even in the churches it most influenced. It was able, nevertheless, to set a tone of commitment and passion that gave many members a reason to give and serve.

Perhaps the most divisive issue is that of the certainty of the outcome. For some Christians the certainty of the eventual victory of the good is the heart of faith. It is the promise that makes acceptance of present injustice possible. For others it is enough that we have hope, and that we know God works with us as we work for justice. The formulation offered above has gone only that far.

We do not know Jesus' thought on this point. Much scholarly debate has centered around the meaning of the Basileia in his teaching. Some place Jesus in the apocalyptic tradition for which a transcendent God would bring about the End without regard to human involvement. Some place him in the prophetic tradition in which the outcome is conditional on human response to the message. These differences divide us still.

The division is critical in those cases where apocalypticists suppose that their participation in the struggle is unnecessary, that passivity is sufficient for us. It is critical also if apocalypticism leads to the view that there is no continuity between what happens now and the Basileia. One might then conclude, for example, with a former Secretary of the Interior, that since the End will come soon we may as well use up all our natural resources quickly. With those who adopt such views there is no basis for collective action or mutual support in diverse approaches.

But apocalypticism rarely leads to that kind of outcome. More often confidence in ultimate victory inspires sacrificial action. Most of the blacks who know that they will overcome, because God is on their side, act with vigor and courage. In that case, those who believe that the outcome depends on human response to the call and those who believe that God will effect it regardless can work together with the Basileia in view. The consensus we seek should be genuinely open to both positions.

A different division may prove more intractable. Some believe that the ongoing course of history is not the arena of salvation at all. The only salvation to be found is here and now in mystical, existential, or psychological experience. The Basileia now in our midst is the only Basileia there will ever be. These Christians may believe that we can find salvation only as we give up future hopes and direct ourselves to present possibilities. Otherwise, they teach, we live by illusions and lose what joy we might find for ourselves and others.

It is difficult to hold in one consensus those who pin their hopes on a future that will reverse much of the present and those who find salvation only in that present. If the latter group opposes all future-directed action, it is better to separate. But many who define salvation in fully present terms see an outworking of that salvation in the multi-faceted service of others. Much of this can be future oriented. Even if the consensus cannot be left open-ended with regard to this issue, present-oriented Christians can be welcomed to stay on as the loyal opposition.

Conclusion
Mutual Conversation as Engaging

Is our sickness unto death? Have we already been spewed out of the divine mouth because of our lukewarmness? Have we used up the capital we inherited from ancestors of genuine faith and commitment?

Perhaps the answer is yes. Perhaps it is too late for us to find a new life and to make a further contribution to God's work for the Basileia. Perhaps we must resign ourselves to the fact that God has found other agents through whom to work.

Nevertheless, this book is written in the conviction that the day of the oldline churches need not be over, that repentance is possible even for us, that our dying churches can yet have new life. It has offered many proposals for how to think and how to act so as to move out of our long decay. It has urged above all that the church take up again its theological vocation.

Perhaps that is a counsel of despair. Our churches are so unaccustomed to thinking that many do not even understand what it would mean to think as Christians. Perhaps the call for theology expresses only the bias of one who chose that vocation many years ago.

Perhaps there is another way of coming alive again. Perhaps there is a way that is in greater continuity with the current style of organization and activity in the oldline churches. Perhaps it is possible to find techniques to gain new members and generate enthusiasm without thinking about our faith and from our faith.

Still, I doubt it. We have been trying that for half a century—just that half century in which we have moved from being mainline churches with some confidence in our message to being oldline churches or, perhaps better, sidelined churches, unclear about our calling. Simply doing better what has not been effective in the past does not seem to be the answer.

The potential resources for becoming thinking Christians are great. In our pews are persons who think a good deal in other areas of their lives. They have not been asked to think about their faith and its meaning for personal and social life. It would not be impossible to ask them to think and even to provide opportunities and occasions to think together.

And if we did begin to think together, what would happen? Perhaps we would simply discover how deeply we disagree. Perhaps we would intensify our quarrels and break our denominations into fragments. Perhaps we would discover how little we really believe, how unimportant being Christian really is to many of us.

On the other hand, there are more hopeful scenarios. Perhaps our thinking would lead to strong shared convictions about the meaning of our faith and the light it sheds on the issues of the day. Perhaps we would be able to address the public with insight and wisdom. Perhaps we could work together for the common good with passion. Perhaps we would find our inner lives renewed. Perhaps we would learn anew the importance of our churches and enthusiastically invite others to join with us.

If we seek the way together, we may find Christ who is the Way. If we seek truth together, we may find Christ who is the Truth. If we seek life together, we may find Christ who is the Life. And the Christ we find will have been the way we have trod in our quest for the Way, the learning that leads to Truth, and the aliveness we will experience as we hunger together for Life.